To: Angela Carlick

A Promise to Persevere:

It's Not Where You Start,
It's Where You Finish

Shun not the Struggle!

Michael Miller

Michael Miller

A Promise to Persevere:
It's Not Where You Start, It's Where You Finish
Copyright © 2006 by Michael L. Miller
and Empowerment Press Publishing Company
All rights reserved

Published by: Empowerment Press Publishing Company

Cover and book design by Yvonne Vermillion, Magic Graphix

Photo by Choice 1 Media

Editorial Director, Andria Cole

ISBN Number 13#: 978-0-9786263-8-9

ISBN Number 10#: 0-9786263-8-9

For more information write to:

Empowerment Press Publishing Company
PO Box 794
Ellicott City, MD.
21041-794
USA
www.apromisetopersevere.com
Printed in Canada

Dedication

The story that follows—all its love, hurt, and inspiration—is dedicated to my parents: The late Dennie Miller who is responsible for all I am and my mother, Nellie Miller, who has waited ever so patiently for my redemption while being gravely ill. Just recently, she told me, "Michael hurry up and write that book. I don't care if I die the day after you finished it. As long as I live to read the final page, my living will not be in vain."

No mama, it won't.

These pages are also dedicated to the single parents of the world and to all of America and Africa's troubled youth trying to overcome life's hurdles and challenges:

Here comes the sun!... brighter days are sure to come!

Acknowledgements

If life is a race, then there must be a coach to help one along the journey. I am fortunate to have been blessed with a variety of coaches who have walked with, supported, or carried me some measure of the way. Many wonderful and powerful people worked to make this project successful, and while it is possible to list each of them, space obligates me to identify only a few and to seek the forgiveness of the many others whose significant names are omitted.

I am humbled daily by God's graciousness and wisdom and particularly by his decision to make me a vessel of change that works to transform the lives of others. Thank you, God, for "ordering my steps." I also respectfully acknowledge those ancestors who fought and died so that I might pursue an education—thank you for guaranteeing my very existence.

And, to my parents, the late Dennie Miller and still-present Nellie Miller, who did the best they could with what they had. Mama, I apologize for all of the times you had to visit the school on account of my behavior, for all of the pain, the headaches, the trials, and tribulations. I hope this is no longer the case, and that, finally, I have given you peace. Daddy, your spirit will always be with me. I apologize for crashing the car—I'll pay you back when I meet you in Heaven. It is because of you I was prepared to follow my dreams. Thank you for giving me the tools I needed to beat the odds.

I am eternally grateful for the support of my children—Dévon, Destiny, and Brianna, who inspire me to take on the task of empowering people to empower themselves. Thank you for being so patient with Daddy, for always bringing sunshine and laughter into my life, and for reminding me why I do what

I do. Thanks for giving me the time and space needed to write this book. Thank you for focusing my life and for making it complete and meaningful.

I want to especially express my deepest appreciation and gratitude for those who have stood with me since the beginning: Rev. Dr. Jamal Bryant for inspiring me to be the man that God intended me to be. Master Eddie Butcher, Grandmaster L.R. Butcher, and Walter Farrar for their encouragement and helping me to engage in the true essence of success through the power of discipline. Mrs. Beverley Arah, a phenomenal, selfless woman with a spirit big as heaven, for consistently and wholeheartedly encouraging me before and during this experience; even though I was "just a G.E.D. student." To my G.E.D. teacher and mentor, Mr. Jonathan White, for picking me up when I had fallen to an unimaginable low. Dr. Tonya Ringgold for her powerful words of wisdom, leadership, guidance and support. Thanks for continuing to push me beyond my measures.

A failing thank you to Oprah Winfrey—for these words lack the gratitude necessary to express just how much your benevolent support has mattered in my life. Thank you for assuming the financial responsibility of my academic matriculation to Morehouse College. Thank you for the enduring words of encouragement you bestow upon your viewing audience daily. It is because of you that so many of us are able to "Beat the Odds."

Though there are many, I sincerely want to thank a few Morehouse Men who have made it all possible for me to attend Morehouse College. I want to personally thank my Morehouse Brother and colleague, Gary Franklin, Jim Henderson, President of the D.C. Morehouse Alumni Chapter. And most of all, I offer sincere gratitude to Dean Sterling Hudson for looking beyond my past faults and failures and for giving me a chance to be considered among the most elite Brothers that any academic institution in the world has to offer — to be a Morehouse Man. Thank you for making it all possible.

I can't forget Little Wayne, who is like a son to me and whom I love dearly. Thank you for your warm spirit and the happiness you showered me with during the realization of this book. And of course, his mom, Lekese Thomas: Thank you for everyday—for the good times and the bad; for the happiness, the laughter, the lessons of love, and most importantly, for literally putting a pen in my hand and demanding that I write this book. Without your push, I would have never done it.

To my surrogate mom, Carol Kellam, for being everything one wishes a mother to be—patient, compassionate, and withstanding. Sorry for crashing your car though! To my sis Nita: Well, what can I say? I thank you, from way deep inside, for everything you have done for me. You are all a brother could need.

To my siblings (Sandra, Jeffrey, Donell, Dennie, Towanda, Kelly, Sheila, and Ronnie): Thank you for your companionship and support, and for sharing this wonderful life with me. Our history and love bind us forever. Special thanks to my big brother, mentor, and confidant, Dennie Jr.: Thanks for being you.

I also thank my editorial consultant, Andria Cole, for her continuous support. Okay Andria, it's done. We can stop fighting now. What a tedious process it has been. Sorry for being such a pain in the neck. You should have known I was going to be a pain from day one! Once again, thanks for all of the aforementioned coaches, for this book would not be without the support and aid of you.

Contents

Foreword

By Dr. Jamal Bryant

There is an old adage that goes, "It's not where you start, but where you finish." Along similar lines, the great philosopher Manuel Diotte said, "Winning isn't always finishing first. Sometimes winning is just finishing." It is important to bear this in mind when dealing with the secular and the sacred—for success in this sphere is not contingent on the start of a thing, but rather on the end of a thing. How great of a man would Noah have been if—after receiving God's directive to build the ark—he stopped half way? How great in Biblical record would any ink be wasted on the life of Nehemiah if upon hearing of his hometown's damaged walls, he started the repairs but stopped when beckoned to come down by the miserable comforters?

It was Sir Roger Bannister, the track and field legend, who once said, "The man who can drive himself further once

1

the effort gets painful is the man who will win." The life of Michael Miller, a former juvenile delinquent, street thug and high school dropout who became a father at the age of 14, perfectly embodies this ideal. He refused to let his circumstances or environment shape his destiny. The story of his life as told in A Promise to Persevere is a masterpiece on the power of the human will.

Like Michael Miller, you will never prove your greatness until you have been trapped with obstacles that seem impossible to surmount. Even when you're feeling down or have experienced some kind of misfortune, you must face these obstacles to get back on the road to your destiny.

Miller proves that greatness is not reserved for a special few. Each of us can envision a better world and do something significant to make a difference. With inspiration and determination, little things become big things. Routine tasks become joyful memorable moments. Simple sentences become inspired messages and stumbling blocks become stepping-stones.

I believe that the human mind and spirit have the ability to influence our physical surroundings and we can use this power to create more meaningful, abundant, and fulfilling lives. We can create virtually anything we want, simply by focusing our thoughts and intentions upon it. The difference between the impossible and the possible is in determination. Motivational speaker Tony Robins said, 'determination is the wake up call of the human will.' I know that I am alive when I am determined. Nothing great will ever be achieved without great people and great people are only great if they are determined to be so. No one is born great.

2

The most empowering thing you can do is to get moving. Don't just sit there and accept what life hands you. Get up, get out and create the life you deserve! Everyone falls but great ones get back up. Don't lie down and cry, roll up your sleeves and get to work. Work is the master key for releasing and maximizing your potential.

Make a promise to yourself that you will continue working toward your goals no matter what happens. Write this promise out and put it somewhere you will see it. Read it aloud to yourself every single day. Keep reminding yourself that nothing will change unless you change it. Fuel your determination with positive thoughts and keep moving forward. If obstacles come up, find a way around them. If there is absolutely no way around a particular obstacle, switch your focus and begin working on another aspect of your goals.

The history of humanity has been filled with tales of the "unimaginable," the "unachievable" and the "certainly not something I'd want to try." Every age, however, is blessed with its heroes - the individuals who ignore their peers and go on to achieve greatness in their chosen endeavor, no matter how daunting the task. Therefore, I am pleased to be one of those people overwhelmed by the Michael Miller story. This is a must read for anyone on a journey to finish something.

Dr. Jamal Harrison Bryant
Founder/Pastor, Empowerment Temple,
Baltimore, Maryland.

Introduction
The Race of Life:
Diminished, But Not Finished!

"The race is not given to the fast, nor the swift, nor the strong, but to he that endured until the end."

-Ecclesiastes 9:11

The scene was Mexico City in 1968. The excitement, which exuded from the watching masses of people was pulsating. If you reached for it, you could hold it. Certainly, you could feel it. A warm, balmy evening, one of many dedicated to the Centennial Olympic Games, was encouraging this vitality.

In honor of the legendary event, Mexico City didn't sleep. Children roamed the streets with groups of friends, imitating their favorite athletes and dreaming of what they might one day achieve. Elders gathered on their porches and storefronts to argue about the day's records and of Olympics past. The spectators who had cheered wildly earlier in the day now reveled in the aftermath. And the media, represented by nearly every country on the globe, worked tirelessly to capture the exhilaration.

Earlier, the Ethiopian runner, Mamo Wolde, was first to cross the finish line in the twenty-six-mile marathon. As he jogged across the finish line, he appeared as fresh as he had when the race started. Behind him, the remaining contenders staggered toward the goal. Some were weary but unhurt; others required medical attention and were rushed to the first-aid stations.

As the day drew to a close, the stadium lights dimmed, the spectators began to leave, and the media crews wrapped up their final segments and sound bites. All that remained was the world-famous Olympic torch — blazing in all its glory.

Suddenly, to the astonishment of the remaining spectators, a lone man stumbled into the stadium. With his right leg broken, bloodied, and bandaged, he hobbled around the four-hundred-meter circuit, wincing with every step. Blood dripped steadily from his elbow. But rather than quit, he tottered relentlessly toward the undulating light of the Olympic torch.

Captivated by this sight — the spectators rose to their feet. With what seemed to be the power of a million hands — they began to applaud him. As he dug deeper into himself and gathered the determination to continue — they applauded. As he summoned the courage to see himself through to the finish line — they applauded. As he continued to stagger and stumble forward with all the energy he had left — they applauded.

6

John Stephen Akhwari, an African runner from Tanzania, had finished last among the seventy-four competitors.

A reporter, sensing an angle for a news segment, chased the exhausted and dehydrated Akhwari. Rather than offering the distressed runner a bottle of water or guiding him to a first-aid station, the unsympathetic reporter thrust a microphone into Akhwari's face.

"Don't you know the race is over?" he asked. "Why, after all this time, would you continue running a race that you couldn't win? Why didn't you just quit?"

The exhausted and visibly pained Akhwari looked straight into the camera and declared forthrightly, "I'm a runner from Tanzania! I didn't come seven-thousand miles to *start* the race. I came seven-thousand miles to *finish* the race!" With that, he limped off the track, oblivious to the thundering applause.

Crossing the finish line a full three hours after the conclusion of the arduous race, the injured Akhwari knew that he didn't have to win; he didn't even have to place. But he had to finish, and that goal had kept him going when every logic in the world simply said, "Quit."

Akhwari understood that in the long run, the destination is far more critical than the paths leading to it. No one would have faulted him for dropping out, given the extent of his injuries. Yet, despite the needlessness, he persevered and finished the race.

Go the Distance!

Before you decide to *"Go the distance!"* you have to ask yourself some very important questions: "What am I running for? What keeps me going in the race of life? Will I give up and stop running my race when I *feel* weary and worn-out?" Chances are, if you're only running life's race simply to run it, you'll be tempted to quit during those painful stretches.

Life is a race. Sometimes it's a series of races (one goal after another) — some won, some lost, some never completed. Many of us never finish our race because we get sidetracked. For one reason or another, people die with unfulfilled dreams, with unrealized potential, without ever becoming what God intended them to be. As always, the prize goes to those who persevere, to those who hang in there to the finish line, and to those who finish strong.

Anyone who has ever completed the grueling 26.2 miles of a marathon will tell you that every inch of those miles is useless if the runner doesn't cross the finish line. Likewise, if while running the race of life you don't see your goals through to completion, you have gained nothing.

Imagine yourself as an athlete. You're in a coliseum just like the one in Mexico City: A field is at the building's center, and seats surround it. The setting is grand, with thousands of spectators to witness the athletic events that will play out on the stage below them.

Life's race is run in a similar setting — a coliseum of sorts. Every seat in this virtual coliseum is filled. Friends, family members, and neutral spectators are seated in the invisible grandstand, watching your race — waiting to see if you will have a strong finish. Past marathon runners who have overcome tremendous obstacles also occupy seats. Though the people in your coliseum's seats may be invisible to the naked eye, they are quite clear to the spiritual gaze.

Can I Get a Witness?

Hebrews 12:1 proclaims: *"In order to finish the race, remember a great cloud of witnesses surround you."* Those who surround us are *witnesses*, not just spectators. The difference between the two is profound. Spectators merely watch you go through something. Witnesses have been through personal trials and tribulations of their own, hardships that mimic yours. Their view of you is supportive; it is compassionate and understanding. These witnesses, despite their difficult ordeals, have found ways to finish their races, and their successes should encourage your victory.

There is nothing like hearing the testimony of someone who has survived a battle similar to your own to bolster your faith and courage. You are better equipped to finish your own race when someone proves that it can and *has* been done. Testimonies empower you to believe that you can finish the race. They encourage you to hold on — and to believe that you will overcome your obstacles. You must always remember the witnesses surrounding you and call on their testimonies to fuel your race.

When I look at the seats around the coliseum where I'm running my current race, I see many witnesses rooting for me: Harriet Tubman and Frederick Douglass, Sojourner Truth and Malcolm X, Martin Luther King Jr. and Fannie Lou Hamer, Marcus Garvey and Mary McLeod Bethune, W.E.B. Dubois and Paul Lawrence Dunbar, Booker T. Washington and Carter

G. Woodson, A. Philip Randolph and Paul Robeson, Benjamin Elijah Mays and Benjamin Banneker, King Shaka Zulu and King Hannibal. Certainly, you have your own list of witnesses who are rooting for you. If you hush the noise of humanity, you may actually hear them. To have your past ancestors cheering for you is to have triumph guaranteed. Remember, "He *who* has run the race before us, runs it now with us."

Like John Stephen Akhwari in the Mexico City Olympics, I made a promise to persevere. I had many false starts, stumbles, and falls, but now, in the prime of my life, I'm progressing. I'm succeeding, not as a man for whom the best is over, but as a runner who is dashing toward the finish line with my eyes on the glorious prize.

Part 1
"We Fall Down..."

"Our greatest glory is not in falling, but in rising every time we fall."
                                                                    -Confucius

Chapter 1
A False Start:
My Humble Beginnings

"Success is to be measured not so much by the position that one has reached in life as by the obstacles which one has to overcome while trying to succeed."

—Booker T. Washington

false start - *noun.* an unsuccessful attempt to begin something.

A stadium hushes. Hundreds of spectators inhale and hold their collective breath. Below them, a single row of 100-meter finalists are preparing themselves for a race that will last about ten seconds. The runners then press their fingertips into the track, placing their hands on the starting line like pool players lining up a break.

Pointing the gun toward heaven, the starter judge yells, "Set!" In one quick, catlike motion, the runners brace their backs and crouch against their starting blocks. Each sprinter is poised and potentially victorious. Each has trained daily, working himself to near exhaustion. Each is the sharpest, the swiftest, and the strongest of his kind. For each, this race is crucial.

But have they trained their minds?

The runner who breaks the tape will need more than physical strength — more than robust muscles — more than a sturdy heart — and more than resilient lungs. He will need concentration, control, and confidence. Ultimately, he must possess an unerring eye for the finish line. One mistimed twitch or slight bend of the knee could trigger a false start and cost any given runner the race. Yet, if he hesitates, if he shifts on the starting block even slightly, his initial steps will lag behind those of his competitors, guaranteeing a loss. "Bang! — Bang!" ... A false start.

Many of us set goals to enhance the quality of our lives, but for one reason or another, we fail to reach the finish line. Maybe you started too soon, like a runner who jumps the starting gun, or maybe you just gave up along the way. If you repeatedly fail to lose weight, to quit smoking, to return to your studies, or to spend more time with your family, the race eventually begins to feel pointless, and for one reason or another, you become unwilling or unable to finish it.

In any given race, if the start is not fair, the starter must declare a false start. In some athletic events, a false start can immediately disqualify an athlete from further competition, but usually the referee will give one warning. This "official" usually determines whether or not a start is a success. If these same principles are what you choose to live by, then the question I must ask of you is, "Who told you that you were disqualified from the race? Who told you that you were worth nothing? Who told you that just because you failed once, you'll never amount to anything? Who defied God's divine order, which declares, *'All things are possible for those who believe.'*?"

If some self-appointed official has convinced you that one false start dooms you to permanent failure, then that "official" is wrong. From a spiritual perspective, your destination in life is not determined by a referee's judgment of your actions. Man does not have the last word. In God's eyes, there is no limit to the number of false starts you can have in life — It's infinite. God always allows us to start over again, regardless of our "false starts."

My Journey

The first of my many false starts was initiated by my humble beginnings. I was born and raised in a sweltering, West Baltimore ghetto called "Sandtown". A small, cramped, three-bedroom row house was home. It was less than four blocks from where the HBO miniseries, *The Corner* took place. My family was the poorest in the community.

In my neighborhood, being book smart meant you were a nerd and, consequently, an outcast. Going to jail and surviving your sentence, however, made you a local hero. Some local criminals went to jail, but many got away

15

with their heinous crimes. The ones who didn't get arrested roamed the streets at night, initiating gang violence, drug dealing, and murders. Somehow, they seemed to elude the local police officers. The crimes, I presume, were far too many for the cops to keep up with.

Most of the people in my neighborhood seemed to glorify the "ghetto fabulous" lifestyle. Dr. Jamal Bryant, pastor of Empowerment Temple, said it best when he once postulated that "ghetto fabulous" is an oxymoron. He concurs that there is no way to be both ghetto and fabulous.

For instance, in Sandtown, there were fragments of broken glass, but we called that "fabulous." The elementary school teachers were often inexperienced and were using four- to six-year-old textbooks, yet we called that "fabulous." We were being charged double for milk, meat, produce, and gasoline, yet we called that "fabulous." The police befriended us but didn't arrest the culprits who were known for selling drugs in our community, yet we called that "fabulous." We celebrated being "ghetto fabulous" and considered it a badge of honor, rather than being a reflection of our destitution.

My mom gave birth to my father's twelve children, five girls and seven boys. I was the baby boy.

The three-bedroom house we called home accommodated many people: my mother, my father, and all their children. My mother and father slept in the front bedroom, my sisters in the middle bedroom, and all the boys slept in the back bedroom in two twin beds, crammed like sardines in a can.

Our bedroom was so small, we had to walk sideways to

get between the two beds. One dresser with two broken drawers held all our clothes. But since we had so few, there was still plenty of drawer space. The vast majority of our clothes were purchased from the local thrift stores, where my mother got nearly everything that our household required: clothes, shoes, lamps, curtains, etc.

The kitchen and bathroom floors were covered in linoleum. The rest of the house had worn-out, painted, hardwood floors that gave us splinters and squeaked as we walked barefoot across them. Some of the floors even had missing planks and revealed the dry, rotted wood beneath.

Paint and plaster were peeling off the ceilings and the walls. In the winter, the cold air constantly whistled through our windows and often wrapped tightly around our bodies. The ceiling leaked whenever it rained. The solution? My mother would just put pots and pans around the house to catch the drips.

Even though the house was small, I will never forget the steel plaque that hung above the mantel in the living room. It read, "Dear God, Bless This House. It May Be Small, But It's Big Enough For Love And That's All." The plaque stood as a monument of faith to inspire us. God's Blessings on the house were far more significant than its size, and His Love kept us warm.

Talk-Back-to-You Shoes

My shoes were what we called, "Talk-back-to-you shoes" because the front "mouth" part was torn and would flap open as I walked. Often, I wore my shoes until the inside soles were worn-out and my feet were touching the ground. As a temporary remedy until I could get new shoes, I would cut some cardboard from boxes and put it inside the shoes, so my feet wouldn't touch the ground. I didn't complain. I was young and poor but always willing to do whatever it took to survive.

We're Marching to Zion

Before we went to church, my parents required us to take part in Sunday morning devotions at 6:30 A.M. We would sing children's songs like, "The B-i-b-l-e, That's The Book For Me." Afterwards, though we were poor, my mother would take the leftover change she'd saved and buy us treats.

No matter how we looked while playing outside, my mother made sure we put on our best clothes before going into "Da House of da Lawd." Just as she did before we left for school, she would line us up and make sure that our teeth were clean, that our faces were washed, and that our clothes were ironed before we left for church.

We belonged to Zion Hill Missionary Baptist Church, which was so small that when our pastor asked, "Would the choir please stand?" almost the entire congregation would stand up. About half of that congregation was my family.

My father held several church offices. He was the church treasurer as well as a deacon, served on the board of trustees, and sang in the church's male chorus.

Consequently, attending church was not an option; it was a

requirement. We would all march in there like an army, taking up two of the four small benches in the church. Whenever we misbehaved in church, my mother would remind us, "This here is da House of da Lawd. Don't y'all be playin' in God's House now, ya hear?" She would always catch us, discipline us, and then go right back to praising the Lord, all within the same breath.

Once, my mom was singing Gospel songs and clapping the tambourine as my brothers and I were playing around. While still on beat, she leaned over, wrung my ears like two wash rags, slapped one of my brothers with her tambourine, then went right back to praising the Lord.

My mother was a gentle, soft-spoken, bashful Christian woman who was generally quiet until you rubbed her the wrong way. When that happened, she didn't have any problem speaking her mind, whether it was to her children, to our relatives, or even to our teachers.

It was my mother who managed the finances with my father's limited income. She was able to stretch my father's paycheck to pay the rent and utility bills, buy clothes when needed, and still have money left over for groceries. One of her frequently repeated adages was, "The Lawd will make a way out of no way, somehow!"

As a wife and mother caring for the household and raising her large family in strenuous circumstances, my mother had to endure all sorts of struggles. Many people would ridicule her, always making her feel like an outcast. They felt that my mother, given the fact that she was so poor, had made a terrible decision to have so many children. No one ever seemed to realize that my father had participated in this process as well. These same people had the audacity to actually ridicule my mother even in her presence. They would say things about her like, "Why would she have so many children? Doesn't she know how poor she is? How can she provide for all of those children? Why doesn't she have a job?" But in the midst of all of the naysayers, she trusted that God would provide, and she gave birth to twelve children.

My aunt and uncle would occasionally volunteer to help raise some of us. They always suggested that they raise the youngest ones, which were Sandra, Jeffrey, and me. However, my mom would entertain no thoughts of anyone else raising us. She intended to keep her family together and ensure that we were raised with the morals, values, and principles to which *she* prescribed.

Sometimes it wasn't so much *what* people were saying about my mom that disappointed her. Rather, it was *who* was saying these things about her that would upset her the most. Some of my mom's closest friends and family members, the same people whom she looked to for moral support, would congregate and criticize her. However, it was her determined faith that God would be a friend to the friendless which sustained her during those difficult moments.

Regardless of the naysayers, she continued to fulfill her duties as a mother, countering the criticism with scriptural references like, "Through Christ, all things are possible." When situations seemed unbearable, she reminded us, "God will never put more on you than you can bear." When the burdens seemed too heavy for her to carry, she declared, "He's my burden bearer, my heavy load carrier." When we were confused about what to do, where to go, or how to get whatever we wanted or needed, she proclaimed, "Ask and it shall be given. Seek and you shall find. Knock and the door shall be opened." Her faith enabled her to endure the strife.

No matter what happened to my mother, or how hard she struggled to raise a family on a small income, her idea of a blessing was simply a new day. She often said, "The true blessing in life is not a new car, a new house, or having lots of money. It is just being able to see a new day. So, every day is a good day! He woke me up this morning and started me on my way! And for that, I'm thankful!"

She would reminisce about how good God is and go into one of her metaphysical moments when she would lift up her hands and cry out, "Thank ya, Jesus! Thank ya!"

Never Walk with Your Back Bent

Whenever my father wanted to call my name, he would start with my oldest brother's name and go through each of my other brother's names in descending order, until, finally, he spoke, "Michael!"

"Ah, Ronnie. I mean, ah... Kelly. Ah... Dennie... I mean, ah... Donnell. No, Jeffrey. Um... Michael. Yeah — Michael. Come downstairs and take out dis here crash (trash) and put 'tin backyard, ah, ri-ri-ri-ri-right now."

Then I'd stutter, "Ye-ye-ye-yes, Daddy."

My father had only an eighth-grade education, but he

wanted the very best for his children. As bad as our living conditions were, he could foresee a better way of life for us, always reminding us that the conditions could "get better than this." A native Southerner full of resilience and determination, he had dropped out of school to provide for his parents.

He worked from 6:00 in the morning until 6:00 in the evening for a construction company. My father drove the company's red bus, which my family affectionately called "Big Red". One of his primary responsibilities was picking up his coworkers in the morning, taking them to work, and then driving them back home at the end of the workday. Dropping everyone off meant that he would occasionally arrive home very late.

Wanting some attention from my father, I often watched and waited for Big Red to come down the street. As soon as I spotted the crimson bus coming over the hump of Fulton Street, I would race down the street and follow it to the bottom of Riggs Avenue, and then into the lot where my father usually parked it.

"Daddy, Daddy, how was work today?" I'd ask.

In a tired, dragged-out voice, my dad would respond, "All right."

One particular evening, when I was about nine years old, I raced down Riggs Avenue to greet him, as usual. He responded in his typically unaffectionate manner, but I didn't care; I desperately yearned for his attention.

Walking with his slow, tired slouch, and back bent, my dad dragged his feet toward our house which stood in the middle of the block. Willing to do anything to get his attention, I started imitating his walk. Suddenly, he looked over and saw me mimicking him. He said in a loud, thunderous voice, "Boy, don'chu evah do dat again. Nevah walk with yo' back bent like dat again. You unda'stand?"

"Yassa," I answered, with tears in my eyes.

"Boy, don'chu evah, and I mean *evah*, do dat again. Ya hear me, son?"

"Yassa," I said again. "But, Daddy," I protested, my voice cracking, "I was just trying to get your attention. I just want to be like you, Daddy."

"Boy, I don't give a damn and don't care, ah, wha-wha-wha-, what-chu say! Ain't no excuse fa-fa-fa-for it! Nevah walk with your back bent over like dat again! I mean it!"

As I straightened my back, I wiped the tears from my eyes. My dad always had said that boys weren't supposed to cry. "Daddy," I asked him, "why can't I walk like you, with my back bent over, too? I was just trying to be like you."

He looked at me with his tired, bloodshot-red eyes and said, "Because, son, when you walk with ya' back bent over, people can ride ya' back. You see, I *have* to walk like this. I can't cry (try) to walk up straight to save my life. But, Michael, ya still young, and ya' got a chance to walk wit' your head up high, with a straight back — With pride!"

I will never forget that moment. Normally my dad stuttered, but on that sunny evening, his words resonated like thunder, and I stood staring at him, stunned by his wisdom. Ever since that day, I have tried to walk with my back straight. The philosophy behind his statement was quite clear. Simply put: "People can't ride your back unless you bend it."

After my dad got off work, he took a shower, ate dinner, and then went to his second job, which was needed so we could make ends meet. At that job, he put his life on the line as a hack, operating as a gypsy taxi in Sandtown. Often, he worked all night for just a few dollars, only to lose those dollars later when he would be robbed at gunpoint. As depicted in *The Corner*, Sandtown was poverty-stricken and rampant with gangs, drugs, and violence.

Normally, the weekend is an opportune time for a son to spend time with his father. However, weekends weren't like that for me as a child. In addition to everything else he did, my father sang with a traveling gospel quartet on the weekends. His quartet was not a big-time group, and they didn't get paid for their services — rather, their performances were considered a ministry, part of their evangelical service to God. Because the group traveled around to sing, my dad stayed busy on the weekends and spent a lot of time away from the family.

Technically, I grew up with my father in my house, but because of his other obligations, he was not home often. Thus, I was almost as deprived as any fatherless child. My father's work obligations made me feel that spending time with me didn't matter to him. Of course, I failed to recognize that he was out providing for the household. Never mind — that he had to sacrifice his time to provide food, clothing, and shelter for himself, his wife, and all their children. Never mind — that without him, my family wouldn't have been able to make ends meet. Never mind — that he was called by God to use his voice to spread the Gospel to others. Regardless of his sacrifices, I still selfishly wanted his attention as soon as he walked through the door every day. I didn't talk about this with my parents or my older brothers and sisters, though, because my family's attitude was that I, as a child, didn't have a voice, much less an opinion. I would have preferred an open relationship in which children could respectfully express how they felt, but in my family, children were supposed to be seen and not heard.

Although my father couldn't give me the attention and affection I wanted, he did the best he could. Besides providing for his wife and children, he was very dedicated to his parents, trekking down to North Carolina whenever they needed him. At times, my father would go to North Carolina every weekend for a month. He supported his parents physically, emotionally, spiritually, and financially. His dedication to the parents who had raised him taught me a lot about truly honoring my own parents.

Like him, I always wanted a better way for my family, but I didn't want to be "a daddy at a distance" as he had been, or struggle to earn a living as he had done. I wanted to be there to watch my future children grow. I wanted to show my children that I valued them, not just with words but also with my actions and a physical presence.

If You Can't Find a Way, Make One!

Both of my parents stressed the importance of finding every possible way to survive. Although there were many obstacles to overcome, my mother never worried about how we were going to make it or how difficult it might be to survive.

She just did what she had to do. As I mentioned earlier, my mother managed our meager finances. My father also found ways to make it. For example, he would steal gasoline by taking a piece of water hose and sucking the gas out of the tank of the company truck. Once the gas started to come out, he would hold the hose over a bucket, and then put the gas in our car. You may call it stealing, but we called it surviving.

Birthdays Were the Worst Days!

My family and I never celebrated birthdays with parties. In fact, the only birthday party that I can remember ever going to was for my buddy, Jay. Though all of us in Sandtown were poor, his mom attempted to give her son a birthday party with the little money that they had. Only six kids attended the party.

For entertainment, we played around his house and in the backyard, just as we normally would do. When it was time to sing "Happy Birthday" and eat some of his birthday cake, his mother presented a small Chocolate Tasty Cake from the corner store. It had a candle shaped like the number ten on top to show his age. The candle was about the same size as the cake. After we all sang "Happy Birthday" together, his mother cut the small Chocolate Tasty Cake into six equal parts, and we ate the bite-sized pieces. It never dawned on us that we were poor; we just ate the cake and had fun.

Mama, I'm Hungry!

Although the people around us were poor, it seemed to my family that they had all the finer things in life. Mrs. Naomi and her two sons, Ricky and Robby, lived in the corner house on our block. She often gave her sons money to buy their dinner from the corner carryout. They would bring home a sub-shop bag that included the usual: a cheese steak or a cheeseburger sub, french fries, and a bottle of soda. You could smell the subs a block away. I used to get upset and think, *Dang, I gotta go in here and eat these neck bones, black-eyed peas, and potatoes, while they eat subs and french fries every day! Man, are they lucky!*

Sure, there were times that we ate well. However, there were also times we had to make due with what we had. In my house, we would fry the bread with lard in a cast-iron frying pan and make "wish sandwiches." You know, the kind where you wish you had some meat. We were grateful for the times we had the big block of welfare cheese. We would take that cheese, slice it and dice it to perfection, put it in the cast-iron frying pan, and make the best grilled-cheese sandwiches ever! We also ate fried bologna, the kind that made a bubble in the middle when you fried it in the pan. I was my own, personal ghetto chef. My specialty was ghetto yat gaw mein. I would take oodles of noodles, boil some eggs, add ketchup, and voila! That was my idea of yat gaw mein.

When there were times that it seemed like there was nothing to eat at all, my mother made a way with what seemed to be no way at all. My mom often whipped up those make-a-way-out-of-no-way meals. She would reach into the, seemingly empty kitchen cabinet, get those welfare, canned meats with the "Not-For-Sale" label on them, and create a piping hot concoction that filled our bellies for the night. I don't know what type of meat it was, or what else she would put into her pot, but whatever it was, it was delicious!

We did have a bit of money for treats, though. When our father came home, he would give each of us a nickel, a dime, or even a quarter to buy some candy. One day, my siblings and I complained to our father that we were hungry. So, he gave us fifteen cents each and told us to go the corner bar to buy a bag of Mrs. Ihries potato chips. We put ketchup in the bag, shook it, and had a meal.

Persistence Pays

As you run the race of life, you will find that persistence pays.

Many years ago, a large, American shoe manufacturer sent two sales reps out to different parts of the Australian Outback to see if they could drum up some business among the Aborigines. Some time later, the company received telegrams from both agents. The first one said, "No business here. The natives don't wear shoes." The second one said, "Great opportunity here. The natives don't wear shoes!" Like the second salesman, we have to learn how to turn lemons into lemonade and obstacles into opportunities, trusting that every setback is a setup for a blessing in your life.

I was a hustler. I learned early to work for everything that I got. From the time I was six years old, I searched for menial jobs on the streets of West Baltimore, walking all over town, running errands to make money. I would walk about a mile from my house to Lafayette Market or even two miles to

Lexington Market just to run errands. Each time, I made sure to come home with something in my pocket.

I even carried bags at the grocery store by asking, "Excuse me, ma'am, may I carry yo' bags?"

"No, thanks. Thanks, anyway," the customer would say. "And what are you doing here, anyway? You're just a baby."

I would persist and say, "Oh, I can carry them, ma'am. I'm seven years old now." Actually, I was only six but determined and persistent.

The woman would respond, "But the bags are bigger than you are."

Assuring her that she didn't have to pay me, that I would carry them for free, I would grab the bags without waiting for a response from the customer.

"Well, since you insist..." and I would follow her to her car. On most occasions, the customer would end up giving me a fifty-cent food-stamp coin, a quarter, or some spare change. I didn't care. I was a little hustler.

At other times, I pumped gas and begged for change at a local Amoco station, "Excuse me, ma'am (or "sir"), can I please pump your gas?" I would ask.

"No, that's okay," they would reply. Just as I did when I was carrying grocery bags at the food market, I would say assertively, "No problem; I'll do it free," hoping that the customer would have mercy on a poor child and give me some spare change. Most of the time, it worked.

Unfortunately, being in a poor community meant that I was surrounded by poor people. Just as they did at the food market, the gas station customers would give me a food stamp coin or a few pennies and nickels. If I was really lucky, I got a wrinkled one-dollar food stamp. "Thank you, ma'am, thank you so much," I would respond. I was grateful, but I was also determined. Every time I went to the gas station, I maintained the faith that I would walk away with something. Even a penny was better than what I had — which was nothing.

At the gas station I learned persistence. I never let a customer tell me "no." Even if the customers didn't want me to pump their gas, I was confident that my charisma would triumph. When they said, "Young man, I'm telling you that I don't have any money to pay you," I would reply, "Listen, you don't have to worry 'bout anythang, sir. I'll take care of everythang." Usually, my charm would pay off and I would walk away with some spare change.

No matter what the weather or the season, I found a way to earn money. If I wasn't pumping gas or carrying grocery bags, I was scrubbing the neighbor's marble steps in the spring, cutting grass in the summer, raking leaves in the fall, or shoveling snow in the winter. If I couldn't find a way, I *made* a way. At fourteen, I began working with temp agencies to make money, telling them that I was sixteen years old, and that I had a work permit.

Be Persistent, Not a Pest

It pays to be persistent, but not to be a pest. Occasionally, persistence can get you in trouble. One time, a customer at the gas station kept telling me "no", and I couldn't take "no" for an answer. I said, "Sir, I'll pump gas. I'll take care of everythang for free." He responded, "Young man, don't you touch my car or dare put gas into it. This is a brand-new Cadillac, and I don't want anybody touching it." I looked at his beautiful, black Cadillac and said to myself, *I know he got some money.*

As soon as he went inside the Amoco to pay for his gas, I heard him boastingly tell the clerk, "Give me a fill up on number two, please." While he was flirting with the clerk, asking her if she wanted to go for a ride in his new Caddy, I grabbed the hose to pump his gas. Seeing a kid riding the bike that I'd always wanted but couldn't afford, a Mongoose, I got distracted. Suddenly, I was unfocused and pumping the customer's gas without permission into what I thought was his gas tank. What was supposed to be a full tank of gas ended up being a brand-new Cadillac full of gas. Gasoline was everywhere. He turned around and shouted at me, "Hey, what in the hell are you doing?" I didn't answer. My heart was beating so fast that I didn't know what to do. I just hauled tail, running and dodging through the alleys hoping to not get caught.

There's Still Hope!

Most of the time, however, persistence leads to success. Most successful people have had more failures than successes, but the more they stumble and fall, the more they pick themselves up and get going again. This is because persistence is directly linked to desire. If you want something bad enough, you will develop the mind-set and energy level to overcome all the obstacles between you and that goal.

The biggest difference between people who succeed and those who don't is not usually talent, but persistence. Many brilliant people give up. Harriet Tubman, one of the most persistent people in history, never gave up on bringing slaves through the Underground Railroad. She gave them two choices: Either escape to the North for freedom or suffer the consequences of death by her rifle. People who are highly successful don't quit regardless of their false starts. Successful people are ordinary people who have fallen down — but have gotten back up again.

Regardless of how many false starts you've had in the past, you must go back to the starting line and begin again. But this time, don't wait for an "Official" to tell you to get your mark. Don't even wait for them to tell you to get set, or to go — just get ready to run, then run. You must possess this type of determination to overcome the false starts in your life.

You must stay in the race! It takes sheer persistence and determination to reach the finish line! I remember once asking my mom, who was cooking in the kitchen, "Mama, what would you do if you were suddenly told that you were going to die tonight?" She replied, "I'm gonna finish cooking these neck bones and black-eye peas so dat when yo' daddy come home, he'll have sometin' to eat." — Now that's determination!

Chapter 2
Lay Aside Every Weight:
Are You a Heavyweight Champion?

"Let us lay aside every weight and the wrongdoings that cling so closely."
—Hebrews 12:1

weight - *verb.* the state of being ponderous, burdened, impeded, oppressed, or handicapped.

It is important to not just know how to get over your false starts, but it's equally important to know how to run your race. If we want to finish the race, we must remove the excess baggage that is on us. I have never seen track stars run with heavy coats on their backs and weights in their shoes. It doesn't take a Ph.D. in aero-dynamics to understand that running with baggage will slow you down. Dr. Brad R. Braxton wrote:

We harbor attitudes and engage in behaviors that wrap around our feet, causing us to stumble rather than to sprint. The writer of Hebrews, Chapter 12 exhorts us to remove these hindrances.

Dealing with Death

Though I was a fast runner who seemed to elude people and circumstances in my life, there were things I couldn't escape, things I couldn't outrun. I've carried a lot of baggage in my life.

Even now, it's emotionally taxing for me to write about witnessing the traumatic deaths of my two sisters when I was three years old. At the time, my mother had just eleven children. My brother Tyrone had died at age one from the complication of Down Syndrome before I was born.

All of my other brothers and sisters were in school that day, except my sister, Shelia. My younger sister, Neicy, and I were desperately waiting for something to eat. So, my mother instructed my older sister, Sheila, who was helping her around the house, to make my favorite meal, hotdogs with pork and beans. I walked into the kitchen with Sheila and my younger sister, Neicy, who was about two years old.

Sheila sat Neicy in her high chair and began boiling the hotdogs and warming up the pork and beans. Neicy was crying because she was hungry, and I was acting out because I couldn't wait any longer to eat. Sheila was going back and forth between the table and the stove, setting up the plate for me, attending to Neicy, and cooking the food.

Sheila chopped some of the hot dogs into bite-size pieces and placed them on the table. As Sheila was walking back to the stove to get the pork and beans, Neicy grabbed and stuffed a whole hot dog into her mouth and began to choke on it. I stood there watching, helplessly, not knowing what to do. It wasn't until Sheila came back to the table that she realized Neicy was choking. She grabbed Neicy and laid her across her lap, repeatedly thrusting her hands into Neicy's mouth, doing everything she could to save her life.

Neicy continued to strain and gasp for air, while Sheila frantically tried to keep her from choking. The more I saw Neicy struggle, the more I cried. To her demise, and our dismay, Neicy choked to death within a matter of minutes. I remember vividly watching without understanding what was happening. All I knew was that I never saw my little sister, who I used to play with every day, ever again.

Family members rushed over to console us. Many of them were especially worried about my mother. After hearing about the loss of a second child, my mother tried to remain calm and copasetic around everyone. Concerned friends and family members would sympathetically ask her, "Nellie, are you all right?" and she would respond, "Child, I'm fine. The Lawd will make a way — somehow." But behind closed doors while my brothers and sisters were in school and family and friends weren't around, I would see her weeping as she worked around the house. Because I was the baby, I saw her crying a lot while everyone else was away.

As my mother cried secretly over the next few months, I, too, began to grieve deeply for the loss of my sister and

35

playmate, Neicy. At three years old, although I couldn't understand where Neicy had gone, I felt guilty, even into adulthood, for just standing there and doing nothing. As a child, I always pretended that I was a superhero who could save the world. There was nothing I could not conquer. If it appeared that someone or something was dead, I thought that my magic wand and superhero powers could save them, just as people were saved from catastrophe in the cartoons. When I realized that I couldn't use my magical beams to make my sister come back to life, I stopped imagining that I had superpowers and could save the world.

I regret that I stopped using my childish imagination to take me beyond my reality. It's always good to imagine things beyond what you can see with the natural eye. Because I was looking at the material rather than the spiritual world, I never imagined that Neicy was with God. She always remained at the kitchen table where I left her, with me standing there, not knowing what to do. I carried this secret trauma for years to come. Just as little Ray Charles stood there in the movie *Ray*, not knowing what to do when his brother died, I, too, had stood idly by.

No, Not Again

Six months after the devastation of Neicy's death, I lost another sister, Jacqualina. I was three-and-a-half years old, and Jacqualina was a newborn baby. I was upstairs with my mother, taking a nap in her bed, where I always slept because it was comfortable. Although Jacqualina's crib was next to my mother's bed, that day she was sleeping with my sister,

Towanda, in Towanda's room. Towanda leaned over Jacqualina to wake her up, and she wouldn't move. I walked into the room to find out what was causing the commotion from my sister screaming. I later learned that Jacqualina had died of SIDS, Sudden Infant Death Syndrome.

Losing two sisters in one year was too much for me to handle. I didn't want to see it happen again. The loss was also overwhelming for my mother, who had given birth to twelve children, only to see herself left with nine.

After the death of a third child, my mother tried to maintain her strength for her children, but the bereavement took a toll on her. She cried a lot about them being gone. Once again, because I was the baby, I was home with her while my brothers and sisters were in school, and I heard her cry and mourn for Jacqualina just as she had done with Neicy. My mother always tried to maintain a tough image because she was raising six boys and three girls who looked to her for strength. At Jacqualina's funeral, my mother suddenly put away the tough image and released her pent-up emotions in front of everybody, screaming at the top of her lungs until she could scream no more. She cried and moaned, "Lawd, why? Please don't take my Jaqualina away from me, Lawd! Neicy just left me! I can't take it anymore! Why, Lawd, why?"

That was a very emotional time for her. I guess any parent would feel that way. She had just lost my brother, Tyrone, a few years earlier, and now she had to face losing two daughters in the same year. As time went by, my mother began to move beyond the deaths of her daughters and to accept the reality that they were gone. She used to say, "God knew that I had too many children, so he called my other three children home." She began to understand that, though they were her Earthly children, they were primarily Children of God. They were put into her life as a loan from him. As Mama gave her problems to God instead of trying to conceal her pain, she began to open up to others about it so that healing could begin, "Weeping may endure for a night, but Joy comes in the morning." From my mother's grieving, I learned two very important lessons.

The first was that you never "get over" the death of a loved one. Many of us imagine that we're going crazy when we just can't seem to get over the loss of someone. But that person was not meant to be someone whom you just get over. Their spirit and memories are meant to be carried with you forever, so that they can be remembered and cherished.

Second, my experience taught me ways to live with such profound tragedy. Grief is an ongoing process with no specific length of time involved. Although the loss and pain will remain, the bereaved eventually learn to live again, to gain control of their lives, and to find meaning in their lives. But this doesn't happen overnight. This process could more aptly be described as recovery — an ongoing process. There is no way to compare our grief with someone else's, and no right or wrong way to deal with it.

According to therapist, Vivian Finlay: "There are, however, what are considered normal or abnormal ways of dealing with grief. Among the normal reactions are emotional outbursts, denial, anger, and disbelief. Abnormal reactions include denial to the point of pretending the loss simply didn't happen."

If the natural reaction to death is not dealt with in normal ways, it can surface in other ways that are more dangerous, such as: alcohol and drug abuse, unchecked anger, or jumping into a relationship in search of replacing your loss. The grieving persons have to face it alone, have to make their own decisions about how their particular path will go, have to feel their own feelings, and have to cry their own tears.

In addition, a big part of grieving has to do with our ability to communicate our feelings. We have to learn to let go and to express what we're experiencing or feeling inside.

According to research conducted by Dr. Ruth Fretts of Harvard University and Dr. Calvin Mackie in his book, *A View From the Roof*, women live longer than men for three main reasons:

1. *A woman will cry.* My mother began to cry to be honest with herself about her feelings. Crying is an emotional cleansing that is good for the soul.

2. *A woman will tell a friend her problems.* My mother began to call up her friends, relatives, and church members to express her feelings.

3. *A woman will give her problems to God.* My mother realized that regardless of how strong she was, she couldn't carry the weight alone without the Power of God. When she tried to carry the weight by herself, the weight impeded her progress. She finally came to the conclusion that she had God-sized problems.

Bad Boy

Another such weight that I've carried even into adulthood is my parents' disciplinary technique. Because my father constantly worked two jobs trying to make ends meet, my mother was the primary disciplinarian. Her version of Christianity encouraged her to "Spare not the rod," which resulted in my receiving daily whippings with a belt, an extension cord, a shoe, a slab of bacon, or whatever my mother could get her hands on the quickest. One beating tool that really stung was the water hose that drained the water from the washing machine into the sink. I used to take her whipping tools and throw them onto the roof of an abandoned building behind our house. When she went looking for something else and grabbed one of my father's belts, I threw all of his belts onto the roof, too.

All my brothers and sisters seemed to have caught on to this old-school parenting technique and have managed to avoid Mom's frequent whippings. But, Michael? No way! I was considered the black sheep of the family — probably because I was the one who always got into trouble.

Although I was disciplined for several different reasons, the primary reason had to do with my education. For example, I would get a bad report card or not get my report card signed by my parents on time. Or I would come home late because I didn't want to get a whipping after I had been bad in school. I would end up getting a whipping anyway because my mom didn't know where I was and whipped me for making her worry.

Don't Beat Me, Teach Me

Nonetheless, as a child, my perception of the beatings was much different in my eyes. To me, there was always someone there to *beat* me for doing wrong, but no one there to *teach* me and show me the ways to do right. My father was overworked, too busy to talk to me about right and wrong because of his work obligations. My mother, too, was busy — tending the house and raising her children. Looking back, I think that my parents' aggression during the disciplining was intended to instill fear in us so that we would do what was right according to God and our parents.

As a result, I learned to respond to fear, and not love. As a child, the only way I could distinguish between the two was by what my parents *showed* me, not by what they *told* me. As a therapist, Dr. Dan Baker, once stated, "Fear impels us to survive, and love enables us to thrive." When a child responds to fear and not love, he or she can suffer a lasting, adverse reaction.

I felt much like how Jose Villegas expressed in his book, *Emotional Prisoner: Trapped Behind the Bars of My Thoughts*, who wrote: "If someone told me they loved me, it felt uncomfortable — uncomfortable to the point that it made me look for ways to escape. When people told me they loved me, I took advantage of them. On the other hand, people who abused me, I bowed down to them."

If our approaches to disciplining our children are not corrected, the devastating effect will be the same as it was with Jose Villegas and myself. These children will take advantage of people later on in life who tell them, "I love you" and look

41

for ways to escape because of the uncomfortable feeling that it brings. However, they will bow down to people who abuse them, as if these people are their slave masters or their overseers.

I believe that I was raised just like many other African-American children, children of any race, for that matter, which is through anger, hostility, and frustration. I'm not totally opposed to corporal discipline. However, I believe that the anger, hostility, and frustration felt by many parents, African-Americans in particular, which they use to verbally abuse and physically discipline their children are the same techniques passed down from slavery prescribed by slave owners. For example, my mother would say things like, "I'm going to beat the black off you." This was a demeaning and derogatory phrase used by the slave masters and overseers that the African-American community unfortunately picked up by default. We just need to be cautious about using such phrases and realize the impact that they will have on our families.

As a result of my many beatings, having witnessed my sisters' deaths, our poor living conditions, coupled with many other stresses while I was still a child, I developed a lot of hatred toward mankind, even toward God, Himself. In fact, I used to curse God, "Where are You?" I would shout, "You're not real! I can't stand You! I hate You! You don't care about me!" I called Him almost every expletive you can think of. I couldn't see what other people were talking about when they said, "God is good all of the time, and all of the time, God is good." I just couldn't understand why God would let a child go through all of this agony.

Because I was taught that boys aren't supposed to cry, I used to act like I didn't care about other people's feelings — when I really did. I was trying to get God's attention. God was hard for me to understand, and I thought no one could understand me.

When my mother beat me, she would say, "Shut up all dat crying, 'fo' I give you something to cry about." So I would stop crying on the outside, while I continued crying on the inside. Therefore, I never stopped crying. Although I would put on my "happy face" for people to see, I was still crying. Although I appeared to be joyful, I was crying. Although tears were not rolling down my face, (on the inside) I was still crying. Consequently, at an early age, I learned not to express my true feelings.

Having this tough image made me bitter at times. To show someone what I was feeling on the inside meant I had to trust them. If I felt like I couldn't trust God, whom I believed to be the Ruler of the Universe, how could I trust mankind or anyone else? I couldn't, so I grew to distrust people in general.

I resented my mother's beatings because they weren't coupled with love and affection. Like many other parents, mine didn't know how to *show* their love. Few of us are masters at parenting, but through trial and error, we can learn the practical skills which our own parents never learned.

One person whom I will never forget is my grandmother. She always showed me a lot of love, care, and concern. No matter how much I was perceived as the black sheep of the family, my grandmother always made me feel special. I think she knew that I didn't get the love and affection I needed because our family was so large.

Whenever she came to Baltimore from North Carolina, she made sure that I got Ritz crackers, while everybody else ate the usual Saltines. This special attention meant a lot to me, as a child who never had the luxury of eating Ritz crackers because they were too expensive. Poor folks in the ghetto ate saltine crackers, which were considered the ghetto version of Ritz. But when Grandma came to town, she made sure that her "Michael" felt loved and appreciated.

This matter of crackers may seem like a small thing, but to a nine-year-old child in desperate need of attention, love, and affection, it meant the world. Looking back, I realize how important it is to pay close attention to the little things, because often it's the little things that make all the difference.

I can't remember my parents telling me that I was loved or special. As a child, I was left to assume that I was loved because my parents provided food, clothing, and a roof over my head. My family was, and still is, very unaffectionate toward each other. Even today, my brothers and sisters don't say, "I love you" to each other, which is something that I look forward to building in the future.

Not until I was an adult did I understand the things that my mother did to demonstrate her love for me. I had to assume that she loved me because she never spoke the words. Children should never have to second-guess whether their parents love them. Many grandparents learn this lesson after their own children are grown. That's why they often try to show *more* love to their grandchildren than they did to their own children.

Case in point: Have you ever noticed that when a mother attempts to spank her children, the grandmother will often step in and say, "Don't you put your hands on that baby!" Many grandmothers know about the importance of love. That's why whenever Grandma comes around, she hugs and kisses her grandchildren, knowing how important affection is to a child. And when you visit her, she makes a special cake or pie just for her grandchild. Grandchildren know that whenever parents can't provide, they can go ask Grandma.

But a grandmother who raises her grandchildren is often stricter than when she raised her own child. Grandmothers have learned from years of experience about how important it is to be involved in a child's life. Research shows that adults who were raised when they were children by their grandparents say that their grandparents were strict, but they later learned to appreciate their grandparents raising them.

Healing with the Words, "I Love You!"

One of the things that I've learned, though, from my parent's discipline techniques, is that words are very powerful. They can either hurt or heal your children for the rest of their lives. Children need to be told several times during the day that you love them. Some parents resist the idea of showing affection within the family. Some parents will even say, "My children know I love them." That may be true, but they need to hear it, anyway. It reaffirms how much you care about them.

The three tender words, "I love you," are critical to children. We often take these words for granted, but I have never known any child to grow weary of hearing them. These words are nutritious for children. Without a consistent dose of saying and hearing these words, the very essence of a relationship between a parent and a child withers.

Your physical presence can also let children know you love them. As the child advocates say, "Children spell *love,* t-i-m-e." They will internalize that you do not love them if you do not spend time with them. If you are always in a hurry, your children will think that you are too busy to pay attention to them. Unfortunately, many of us are proactive, rather than reactive to spending time with our children. We wait until it is too late.

Say It with Feeling

It's not what you say; it's how you say it. According to psychiatrist Katherine Wisner, the words we use make up only about ten percent of the communication process. Paralinguistics, the way we say the words, makes up forty percent. But the remaining fifty percent consists of nonverbal features — what we do with our face, our body, and our hands as we're speaking.

The rhetorician Kenneth Burke once said that words don't have meaning unless you give them meaning. The difference between a reluctant "I love you" and an affectionately said "I love you" is the difference between a confused child and a happy one.

Healing with a Hug

Many of us don't hug our children enough. They need to be hugged every day. And if the truth were told, you need it every day, too. Every day, before your children leave the house, give them a big hug, look them straight into their eyes, and tell them, "I love you."

When you are hugged, your body releases chemicals called endorphins that make your body feel good. These endorphins increase your resistance to diseases and help to reduce pain. Never underestimate the power of hugging. Hugs are not only nice, they are needed!

Help Carry the Load!

You can help your children avoid having to carry the everyday load of peer pressure by communicating your love and understanding in words, your physical presence, and your hugs. As parents, we often underestimate the pressures that children have to face in school and in the community. You can say something as simple as, "Look, I understand the amount of peer pressure that you may go through in school; however, I want you to know that I love you to death! I know the stuff that you face every day is big stuff, but I want you to know that my love for you is way bigger than that!" This kind of communication is critical in helping to prevent your children from carrying the load from their childhood that they could never communicate to you before. It may even determine whether they join a gang or end up doing drugs.

Let it Go!

Regardless of what you've been through in your past, you must lay aside the weight that you carry. Many of us are still carrying the weight of the loss of a loved one, having an unforgiving spirit, an old grudge, or an old relationship. Today is a good time to remove what is on us in order that we might run more swiftly.

On the other hand, what may be a weight to one person may not be a weight to another. Therefore, we must occasionally ask ourselves the question: "Is it a *wing,* or is it a *weight*?" The things that we carry must be a benefit, not baggage. We need to know whether it speeds us on our way to our destination, or whether it slows us down. We can be so overwhelmed by failure that we just stop running. We just give up because giving up is easy. However, we must be in the race for the long haul — in spite of the obstacles or the difficulties. Remember, you are *not* running a short dash; you are *running* a marathon!

Chapter 3
Troubles in My Way:
School Daze

"Education is our passport to the future, for tomorrow belongs to the people who prepare for it today."

—Malcolm X

trouble - *noun.* a state of distress, affliction, or difficulty within any given circumstance or situation.

D espite poverty, despite destitution, despite deprivation, my parents' commitment to my education stood resolute. As an active and passionate member of the Parent Teacher Association, my mother never missed a report-card night or an after-school assembly. She was unswerving in her determination to be a force in my education, and I often imagined her looking over my shoulder, checking my assignments or questioning my behavior.

49

My father was illiterate, which made him even more adamant than my mother about the importance of education. He would often ask either my mother or one of his children to read his mail.

"Hey, Michael, come read dis here mail fo' me."

"I don't know what it's saying, Daddy," I would tell him, "but I think you owe dem some money."

"Is it a bill collector?" he would ask.

"Yassa. I think so."

He'd reply, "Well, hell, if it ain't a check, I don't wanna see it!" Then he would ask, "Well how much do I owe?"

"I think it says here you owe three-hundred dollars."

Then he would get hysterical and shout repeatedly, "Three-hundred dollars! Three-hundred dollars! — Well, call dem and tell dem I ain't got it!"

Then he'd go off and have a temper tantrum, "Every time I turn around, seems like the bills keeps coming! Boy, call dem and tell dem I give it to dem next week, when I get paid!"

Then I would call the bill collector and say in my childish voice, "Yeah, ah, bill collector, my daddy said he ain't got da money, and he give it to you next week when he get paid." Then I'd hang up the phone.

As always, when he would get paid the following week, he would pay off his debt. He was an honest man. He didn't believe in owing anybody money. He would often say to me, "Hey, Mi-Mi-Michael, ma-ma-ma-make sure you ga-ga-got to g-g-go to school and work. You understand?"

I'd respond, "Yassa."

He would continue, "G-g-go to school and git yo'self a good job. Matter 'fact, a good gov'ment job."

"Gov'ment? What's that, Daddy?"

He would raise his voice and say, "Bo-bo-bo-boy, you know what da hell I'm crying (trying) to say! Go to school and git yo'self a good gov'ment job! You understand?"

"No, Daddy," I would respond. "I'm gonna to get lucky and be rich. I ain't working like dat every day! I ain't got to go to school. I'm gonna get lucky."

My father didn't believe in luck. "Boy, ain't no su-su-su-such thang as luck! I found out that the harder I work, the luckier I get! You ga-ga-ga-got to go to school so you can get a good job and pay yo' bills."

Even in a family as poor as ours, my parents always stressed the importance of doing well in school, so that we could get a "good education." My mother made it clear that if she ever had to come to the school to meet with a teacher, principal, or other authority figure, it had better be because we'd done something good. These rules of school discipline seemed to work well for my brothers and sisters, but once again, not for me.

If you asked any of my teachers what kind of student I was, they would all say that I gave them a lot of hell! From kindergarten through high school, I kept my mother busy going back and forth to the school on my behalf. Far too often, my mom was called to rectify some infraction of mine, some breach of school rules. She would storm through the school building's doors with me in mind, and march back through them with me in tow. I just couldn't seem to shake my disobedient cycle in school.

I always wanted to be the class clown, because being disruptive was a way to camouflage my illiteracy. I also wanted to be the center of attention at all times, no matter what the cost, because I wanted to fit in with the "In crowd". That way, the attention would be on my bad behavior and not my poverty. As a consequence, I consistently received failing grades.

I was sent home almost every day for acting out in school. I knew I was going to get a beating whenever I was sent home without my mom. This made my walk home the longest walk ever. The four blocks between the school and my house swelled to fourteen. And suddenly, a five-minute walk lasted five hours. I couldn't stomach the thought of her greeting — short on hello, and long on whipping — so I slowed my pace and let my feet drag where they would usually be strutting. Suddenly the neighborhood was more colorful, more interesting, and needed to be meticulously viewed. The beating, despite my tourist-style walk, always awaited my arrival.

Usually my mom had already received a phone call outlining my behavior, before I even reached the house's threshold. And as soon as I walked through the door, her whipping tool was upon me, and my body was bruised with welts. Yet, nothing — not my mom's belt across my behind, not my dad's words slapped angrily against my ears, not my teachers' looks of disdain when I entered the classroom — deterred my actions. My behavior wouldn't be changed for nearly two decades.

My mother puzzled herself many times, trying to figure out what was wrong with me. "Why does Michael have to be the class clown all the time?" she would wonder out loud.

"Why do I have to keep going back and forth to the school almost every day? Why does the school have to keep sending him home because of his behavior?"

Michael the Menace

My third-grade teacher, Mrs. Sanders, collected notes on my disobedient episodes and stored them where they could be retrieved easily. She seemed to keep my disciplinary history in her front pocket and recovered it whenever we interacted. I could never look forward to a new day with Mrs. Sanders, because for her I remained the same Michael from yesterday — a menace. Each morning she greeted me with a drawn out "Good... morning..." and faithfully affixed her assumptions and disgust to that salutation. While I claimed the vast majority of her classroom disruptions, to her, I was a menace, so I had to wear that title, come rain or shine.

One particular morning exemplified this branding. My mom was downstairs in a parent/teacher conference to discuss some trouble which I had gotten myself into just a couple of days prior in another classroom disruption. My classmates were being very rowdy and misbehaving. Mrs. Sanders was writing the day's assignment on the chalkboard. While her back was turned, my classmates began to shoot spitballs across the room. Mrs. Sanders stopped writing and looked around to see who was causing all the commotion. She assumed it was me, but on that particular day, it wasn't. I had just gotten into trouble from a couple of days before and my hind parts were still sore from last night's whipping.

She then pulled my long disciplinary history from her front pocket, and, without even turning from where she stood, she yelled, "Michael, why are you shooting those spitballs across my room?"

I replied in a shocked voice, "It wasn't me, Mrs. Sanders!"

She said, "It was you! Now, get over here!"

I sauntered through the aisles of the classroom with my thrift-store jeans and my brand-new, K-Mart-fabulous shirt. I was looking just like I was half-thrift store and half-brand-new. I remember that shirt fondly. It had colorful stripes and a red collar. That shirt instantly became my favorite because it was store-bought, and it was so seldom that I would get brand-new clothes. I was unusually clean on that day, too.

I trotted over to Mrs. Sanders with the welts from yesterday's beating still stinging my backside, and with absolute certainty that I would be believed. After all, my mom sat only one floor below Ms. Sanders' classroom in a parent/teacher conference. Surely, Mrs. Sanders knew that I was sharp enough not to disturb her class while my mom was downstairs at a parent/teacher conference! I was unruly — not stupid.

Mrs. Sanders grabbed me by the collar and yanked me so hard that she ripped the collar off my shirt. Boy, was I upset! As she yanked me, she uttered those verbally-abusive words that many teachers were notorious for using back then. Mrs. Sanders said to me, "You must not get enough attention at home!" That saying was commonplace inside our classroom walls, and it served a dual injustice: to silence the child, but also to humiliate him.

Although she may have been right, given the size of my family and our circumstances, I felt like she had no right to say those words. To make matters worse, the entire class burst out laughing at her comment. Instantly, the tables were turned. I had gone from class clown to laughingstock. I had been both violated and humiliated.

Back then, the intercom system was set up so that teachers could call from the classroom to the main office. So Mrs. Sanders, knowing that my mom was in the building, walked over to the intercom and called the office where my mom was having the parent/teacher conference, and she strongly advised, "Mrs. Miller, you need to come get your son and teach him some home training."

Mrs. Sanders then ushered me out of her classroom and demanded that I go to the first floor and find my mother. Needless to say, my mom was quite embarrassed. Wearing a bright flush all across her face and neck, she started on a rampage of her own when she saw me, waving her hands and arms in a blind fury. Rather than question *my* behavior, she said that Mrs. Sanders was being too "sassy." Then my mom took me by the hand and hurriedly walked me back to Mrs. Sanders' classroom, all the while going off on Mrs. Sanders. She kept repeating that Mrs. Sanders was being too "sassy." I listened to her seething with a clamped-shut mouth.

That's Not Even A Word

As she frequently did back then, my mom threw in a couple of made-up words, "I ain't gonna have no *pristalistic* woman put her hands on my son. She must have lost her mind! Dat shirt cost me three dollars and ninety-nine cents. We don't have a bunch of money to be *frubalistically* throwing away. I ain't gonna have nobody disturb me in an *innoventabuttous* manner while I'm in the parent/teacher conference. I got neck-bones, black-eye peas, and collard greens on da stove, and now she gon' make me late. Shoot! I've been nice to her since day one, and I ain't gonna have it no mo'!"

By the time we reached the top of the stairs, we stood breathless at Mrs. Sanders' classroom door. My mom opened the door to signal Mrs. Sanders to step out into the hallway. Then, my mom assumed her humble Christian posture: She tilted her head slightly to the side and laced her fingers together as if to begin a prayer. Then, from her mouth came a perfectly soft voice, completely unlike the riotous one she displayed during her irate trek up the stairs, "Mrs. Sanders, excuse me, could you please step outside the door?"

Mrs. Sanders joined us with an annoyed look on her face. Then — my mom let Mrs. Sanders have it. "There are several things 'dat I would like to speak to you about dis afternoon. Number one, don't nobody put their hands on my son but me, okay? Dat shirt cost me three dollars and ninety-nine cents. And don't you evah call where I am and disrespect me again! You unda'stand? You make sure dis is the last d@mn time you evah get sassy wit me. But I'll tell you one d@mn thang. Call down there again and see what happens, I dare you!"

Whenever my mom was around teachers and she couldn't exactly express her point, she would be compelled to make up words to sound intelligent. The teachers would look at her strangely, trying to figure out the meanings of the strange words rather than what she was trying to say. For example, she was telling Mrs. Sanders about being "sassy," which was commonly used around my household when we kids were talking back to a grown up or trying to be above ourselves. However, what my mom really meant was that she was being 'sarcastic.'

Things might have remained purely verbal and nearly orderly, had Ms. Sanders not belittled my mom. My mom, in an effort to appear intelligent, said, "And don't you get sassy and *sissyfalicoulteniusous* with me, young lady. Oh, no!"

Mrs. Sanders responded in a very condescending voice, "Hey, that's not even a word, Mrs. Miller!" Before the smirk had settled on Mrs. Sanders' lips, my mom was on top of her, beating her down on the floor, much like one of her own children.

I immediately ran to the main office to tell someone that my mom, a devoted PTA member, had stomped my third-grade teacher like a mere bug, just one floor above. By the time I arrived at the main office, I was totally out of breath. I gasped out, "(Huh, huh, huh,) excuse me, my mom, ah, my mom, is upstairs."

Before I could finish, the school secretary said, "Huh?"

Trying to catch my breath, I said, "Ah, my mom is upstairs, beating–"

"You will have to wait your turn," she interrupted. "Now, get somewhere and sit down!"

I said to myself, *What?* The secretary's refusal to recognize the fear in my shaking voice and sweating face infuriated me. Since she wanted me to wait, I sat and waited for ten long minutes while my mom was upstairs, beating the living hell out of Mrs. Sanders!

When the news finally got back to the main office, the faculty, teachers, and administrators came from all over the building to break up the fight. Back then, they didn't have school police officers in elementary schools, so no one could control her. My mom was in the middle of the hallway, yelling, "Yeah, call the police! I ain't scared of no police! Call the police!"

My mom had a very good relationship with the principal, a White man named Mr. Walpert. He was a polite man who respected my mom for raising nine children, all of whom went through Gilmore Elementary School, with Mom being actively involved in the PTA. He frequently drove her home after the PTA meetings, instead of letting her walk home in the dark.

When the police finally arrived to lock my mom up, they started to manhandle her even though she was being humble and making no attempt to resist arrest.

Meanwhile, I was crying and shouting, "Get your hands off of my mama!"

Mr. Walpert intervened, "Now, wait just one cotton-picking minute, buddy!" he said to the policeman who was about to handcuff her, "Don't you guys dare disrespect and put handcuffs on her! And stop mishandling her like she's some criminal! She is a lady, a decent, law-abiding citizen who is actively involved in the PTA meetings here and has sent her nine children through this school! Now, take those handcuffs off her immediately and treat her like the person she is — a lady! So respect her as one!"

I will never forget that moment. I was delighted at what Mr. Walpert had said. The administrators were amazed. The cops were confounded. The teachers were traumatized. Here was a White man, in his position, adamantly standing up for the civil rights of a Black woman. Immediately, the foyer fell silent. The cops obeyed Mr. Walpert's commands. One of them got on his radio and requested a policewoman to come down from the precinct, which was only one block away. She arrived quickly, taking the handcuffs off my mom and putting fingercuffs on her instead, then she escorted my mom out of the building to the police cruisers.

I stood there in the foyer, crying as loudly as a baby with tears rolling down my face, thinking that I would never see my mother again. Filled with anger and frustration, I despised everyone around me and blamed them for my mom being taken away. As the administrators tried to calm me down, I retaliated with mean and hateful words. I wanted them to feel what I was feeling.

I sat in the main office asking myself, *What happened? My church-going, spirit-filled, Christian mother had lost her mind and beat up my teacher!*

It wasn't until about an hour later that I finally calmed down, with the assistance of Mr. Walpert. He assured me that everything would be okay. And, for some strange reason, I believed him. He called my father on his job and asked him to come pick me and my brothers and sisters up from school.

While we were home, I waited all night long, wishing and hoping for my mother to return from jail. I must have cried a million tears waiting for her return.

"Michael, stop all dat crying," my father said. "Yo' mama

gonna be just fine! Y'all chil'ren need to learn how to have some faith. God didn't bring us dis far to leave us now. Shoot! If it wasn't fo' the Lawd, we wouldn't have all the thangs we got now!"

I would respond to myself and say, *Daddy, we ain't got nothing!*

Then my father would walk away, singing one of his favorite gospel songs for inspiration, "If it had, not, been, for the Lawd, on my side, tell me where, would I be; (whoa, yeah!) where would I be?" My father then left the house, to return home with my mother late that evening. Being just a child, I had thought she would never get out of jail, but I was finally relieved of my desolation.

Following the fight between my mom and Mrs. Sanders, my brothers and sisters and I had to be transferred from Gilmore Elementary to Matthew A. Henson Elementary. I instantly fell in love with my new school. After lunch, we had recess when we went outside and played for half an hour. We ate with stainless-steel forks and spoons, and porcelain plates and trays, not the plastic spoon-forks and Styrofoam plates that we used at our previous school. Of course, the transition was a bit difficult because my friends weren't there, but I got used to it.

During the first week of school, I immediately made a name for myself as the new kid because I felt like I had to act out to fit in with the "cool" kids. I became disruptive in class and picked on other students all day.

Meanwhile, my mom was facing a ten-year sentence for assault and battery. She walked boldly into the courtroom without a public defender or a hired attorney, steadfast in her faith in God and confident that she could represent herself. She just quoted one of her usual adages, *"He's* a lawyer in the courtroom." Even though my mother had faith in God and solely depended on Him to get her through her trial, I didn't. I sat in the courtroom, worried the entire time that she would go to jail.

When it was finally time for my mother to approach the courtroom podium, the judge said to her, "I would send you to jail, but you have so many children that I'm afraid they would be raised without a mother." Then he asked her, "Mrs. Miller, are you sure you can raise all of these children?"

My mom replied with certainty, "Yes."

The judge gave her one-year of probation.

Needless to say, I was elated by the judge's decision.

To Be Popular or to Be Smart?

Most of my failure in school resulted from trying to be popular rather than smart. My teachers complained about my low math and reading skills. To improve my math skills, my mom made me memorize all of the numbers on the multiplication table found on the inside cover of my black-and-white composition book. Every day, my mom and I went over the table, over, and over, and over, again, until I finally knew the table by heart — all the way through the number twelve.

Because of my disruptive behavior and illiteracy, the teachers tried to put labels on me. I remember overhearing them say that they wanted to put me in a Special Education class, which was called D.E.C. (Department of Exceptional Children) back then. Kids would tease students in D.E.C. classes and say that it stood for Dumb Educated Children. I would rhetorically ask myself, *How can you be dumb and educated all at the same time?* I guess kids say the darnedest things.

The learning-disability labels that the teachers thought were appropriate for me were LD and ED, meaning "Learning disabled" and "Emotionally disturbed." Marian Wright Edelman, a social reformer, once said, "Parents have become so convinced educators know what is best for children that they forget that they, themselves, are really the experts." My mother held the same belief. Regardless of my hyperactive behavior and poor performance in class, she fought those stigmas and rejected those terms by saying things like, "Nothing is wrong wit' you, Michael. Dem teachers up at dat school don't know you." My mom, who was an ardent biblical scholar, began to quote Scriptures and remind me once again, "Through God, all things are possible." She always knew just what to say from the Bible in times of need.

Dr. Jawanza Kunjufu, who wrote, *To Be Popular or to Be Smart,* said that before the fourth grade, the average African-American child has the intellectual aptitude to do well in math and in science. But by the time they actually get to the fourth grade, they are reading two grade levels below where they should be. This is not because African-Americans are intellectually challenged, but it is because many of us consciously make the decision to be popular rather than smart.

Many young people make the same mistake I did, choosing to be popular in school rather than making smart decisions. At some point, each young person has to ask themself, *"Do I want to continue to be popular or do I want to be smart?"* Indeed, this problem is not limited to the young, African-American population; this is a problem with young people in general.

Middle-School Gang Wars

After elementary school, I went to Lemmel Middle School, a very tough and disruptive environment where students were rude and disrespectful. There were gang fights every day on the bus to school, in school, and after school. It was normal for a seventh or eighth-grade student to bring to school a .22, a .32, a .38 automatic, or whatever type of weapon they could get their hands on. When guns weren't available, students carried knives to protect themselves. Because it was the only way to survive, I, too, developed the mentality of a juvenile delinquent.

Many of us spent our time in woodshop class carving sticks to fight with or hard, plastic knives to use as daggers. Lemmel Middle School students often rivaled with Frederick Douglass High School. Lemmel Middle School would go to Douglass High School to fight their students and vice versa. Toward the end of my sixth-grade year, I was expelled from Lemmel Middle School and sent to Calverton Middle School to finish the year. I didn't know it then, but God had a plan for me. He was ordering my steps.

A Father at Fourteen

I lost my virginity while attending Calverton Middle School. It happened on my fourteenth birthday with my girlfriend, whose name was Candy. She and I were the same age. It was evident that I had a sweet tooth for her, because I came around her house looking for her every chance I got. One afternoon, Candy's foster-mother, Mrs. May, walked her to my house to talk to my parents. I was in my mom's room at the front of the house, watching the scene and gauging their reaction.

My mother answered the door and assumed her normal Christian pose — an erect back, arms resting politely at her side, chin lifted just enough to signify her pride in her uprightness.

"Hello, may I help you?" she asked.

The woman at the door was tight-lipped and determined. She said, "Good evening. My name is Mrs. May, and I just want you to know that your son, Michael, well, he got my foster-daughter pregnant."

Those words hit my mother good, right between the eyes; she tensed and made fists with her hands. Just as she had done with my third-grade teacher, Mrs. Sanders, she quickly came to my defense. Only this time, I really was at fault.

"Oh, no! Not my son!" she said, fighting back tears. "You see, my son goes to Zion Hill Missionary Baptist Church *every Sunday,* where the Reverend Goode is a very fine pastor! He is a child of God; yes, he is. My son is saved, baptized, and washed in the blood of the Lamb!"

She stopped to breathe and take in Mrs. May's words. The two women looked at each other. Obviously, neither wanted the words to be true, but one, Mrs. May, was much closer to believing them than my mother.

"Besides, my son is only fourteen years old, you know?"

My mother started up again, this time seasoning her talk with those made-up words so comfortable in her mouth, "There is no way my son could have *fertilaciously* and *impregnatatiously* fertilized a baby into your dawta. He is just a baby, Mrs. May! He's still wet behind the ears."

Mrs. May replied, "Mrs. Miller, your son, Michael, ain't all what he is cracked up to be. There were plenty of times when I had to run him away from my door, because he was around my house so much. He was always coming around, looking for Candy."

"Now hold on there, Mrs. May," my mother interjected. "I just don't know how true that is. One thang I know about my son is that if he wanted some candy, he would've earned his own money to buy his own candy. He would've went round the corner to the market to carry them people's groceries. He would've pumped some gas at the gas station, or cut somebody's grass to get his own money to buy his own candy — 'fore he went begging you for some."

Had things not been so serious, Mrs. May might've laughed at my mother's confusion. But things were serious, and Mrs. May was growing impatient.

"Oh, Mrs. Miller, you don't understand–" she began.

Before the woman could explain that "Candy" was her daughter's name and not a lollipop or ten-cent taffy, my mother interrupted her and talked over her words with bigger, purely invented ones, "Oh, no, I understand, all right. I understand y'all trying to put a *conspiracitation* on my son; that's what I understand! Y'all trying to set him up, saying that Michael *fertilaciously impregnatized* yo' dawta! But that shall not be the revelation here today. *Thus saith the Lord, thy God*! Because the Bible says" — and here she closed her eyes to let

65

the mighty spirit fill her — "Touch not my anointed and do my child no harm!" She punctuated those words with a slight lift of her already-raised chin, and there she remained — chin raised, eyes shut so tightly that no light could seep in.

"Mrs. Miller" — Mrs. May ignored those closed eyes — "please relax. You see, I'm not talking about the kind of candy that children eat. My daughter, Mrs. Miller, my daughter's *name* is Candy!"

My mother let those words settle on her. They must have held meaning, because she peeled back her eyelids and held her tongue still. She regrouped and allowed Mrs. May to have her say.

After the woman had said her piece, my mother cleared her throat and smoothed her dress with the very hands that only seconds before had been fists.

"I'm sorry, Mrs. May," she said. "I'm so sorry. Well, okay, then. I'll be sure to tell his daddy when he gets home."

For every word my mother invented, my father stuttered three or four. When the frustration was too big, when it bubbled within him and made a mess of his thoughts, no one, not even himself, could understand what he was saying. And learning that I'd gotten a girl pregnant at fourteen was one of those situations.

"Hey, Micka, Mmm-mm-Macka!" My name was a bundle of confusion on his tongue. "Ma-ma-ma-ma-Macka, ge-ge-ge-get down here, r-r-r-r-ret now!"

As soon as I came downstairs, I responded, "Ye-ye-ye-ye-yes, sah?"

My father instantly began to chew me out, "Now wha-

wha-wha-what in da hell you go off and, uh, get some gal pregnant fo'?" He paused to take a breath and started up again, "I tell, I tell ya, I tell ya, boy, I tell ya, tell ya, ya-ya-ya-ya-ya." He paused, took a breath to sigh "Phew!" and then wiped the sweat from his forehead. "You ain't got two cents worf of good sense! I tell ya one thang, ya gonna get a job and work. You ain't si-si-si-sittin' around da house. Ya gittin' da hell outa here. I tell you, boy, ya ca-ca-can't, can't, can't, can't do nothing right. Every time I turn around, ya always into something, ya knotty-headed rascal! Why can't ya do good like da rest of da chil'ren?"

Contemplating Fatherhood

After the lecture from my father, I knew that having a baby meant serious business. My father didn't believe in abortion. He had taken on the challenge of raising his twelve children. Nor did the idea cross my mind, possibly because I was still a child myself.

We were fourteen-year-old babies about to have a baby, a circumstance that neither of us was mentally, emotionally, educationally, or financially prepared for. The thoughts running through my head scared and confused me, *How do you take care of a baby? What am I supposed to do if it cries? Where is the money going to come from? How do you love a child? Do you beat them when they do wrong?* It was emotionally draining even to attempt to answer those questions. I was carrying an adult load on a child's back, and the weight was too much for me to bear. In fact, neither of us took it seriously enough to prepare ourselves. I remember being very afraid.

My solution was to run away from my responsibility as a father. As the pressure increased, I gradually stopped wanting to be around her. Suddenly, I didn't have a sweet tooth for Candy anymore.

Toward the end of her pregnancy, when she was visiting my house, I finally confronted her and told her exactly how I felt, "Candy, this is too stressful for me. What am I gonna do? I don't have a job, and we still live with our parents. I hardly see you because you've moved to the other side of town. So, I just think it's best that we just break up."

She looked at me sadly and said, "Why would you do something like this? Don't you think that it's hard on me, too? Michael, I don't want to lose you."

I responded childishly, "I don't want to lose you, either, Candy, but, hey, a man gotta do what a man gotta do."

Her sister called her, "Candy, c'mon; it's time to go home." As she walked away, she looked at me in confusion, knowing that she would have to carry the bulk of the adult load by herself, without my assistance as a father or as a boyfriend.

I just stood there, hurt, lost, and confused as to whether I was making the right decision, and holding back my tears as she walked away from me. I felt that I was leaving behind a friend whom I could talk to about anything that was going on in my life. Now I had to bear those burdens by myself, all because I was scared of being a father, scared of being responsible for a life other than my own. I could barely take care of myself with the help of my mother. I ran the streets and taught myself how to survive.

Failing as a Father

Of all of the things that I've regretted in my life, I regret most not being a father to my son during his infancy.

After my son, Dévon, was born, I continued to hang out on the streets with the wrong crowd. I often felt bad, knowing that I was running away from my responsibility, but I had many outside influences encouraging me to do the wrong thing, and very few people to *show* me how to do better. Consequently, I failed as a father to Dévon, and I failed as a friend to Candy. My priorities as a fourteen-year-old child were to run the streets, hang on the corners, and to party. The people around me were incapable of modeling effective parenting; I could not learn how to be a father from any of them. They would often deny their child and say, "Dat ain't my baby."

When it came to fathering my son, there was nothing in my community or household to inspire me. I thought I could be a daddy from a distance. Even though Candy and I were no longer a couple, my father expected me to be a responsible parent to my son. He believed, firmly, that if you have a baby, you have to take care of it. But because my father worked most of the time, he couldn't oversee my activities. He would come home and ask, "Boy, did you go see your son today?"

I would respond with a lie, "Yassa!" When Dévon was about a year old, Candy brought him around to see me. After that, my dad would go and get him occasionally and bring him to the house. Usually I wasn't at home. When I was, I didn't know what to do, what to feel, or what to think. I wanted to be a father and to show my son the love and affection that a father should show, but I didn't know how. So, I chose to hit the streets more than anything else. After a while, it became second nature. Besides my father's earnest attempts, there weren't many loving fathers around me to inspire me, none that I was conscious of, anyway.

But Dévon was not the only child that I neglected to be a father to during my early teen years. When I was seventeen years old, I got my girlfriend, Nikki, pregnant. I knew I was the father of her child, but I responded as usual, "That ain't my baby!" She too, felt the wrath of my juvenile and insensible ways of failing as a father. I actually was there at the hospital when my daughter, Brianna, was born, which made me a little more attached to her then anyone before. However, it was after she was born that my failure-as-a-father rampage created havoc for me to see her as often. Nikki couldn't divulge all of her trust with leaving her with me as often because of my impulsive, juvenile behavior.

One day I was high from smoking marijuana, and I left Brianna in the house by herself with my nine-year-old nephew to watch her while I was hanging out in downtown Baltimore. Nikki soon found out, when she called my house, from my nephew that I was not there. I called her while I was out. She then told me that she was on her way to my house with the police. I rushed back to the house and got there just in time before Nikki and the police arrived. The police continued to bang on my door and said, "Mr. Miller, open the door, NOW!" As I took another puff from the weed I was smoking, in my childish ways, I responded, "You can keep on knockin', but ya' can't get in!" Then I started singing out loud in front of the door so they could hear me, "I shot the sheriff, but I didn't shoot the deputy!" Meanwhile, my newborn baby started crying from the constant bangs on the door. I finally opened the door after the continuous banging and let them take her away. And just as with Dévon, I was not there as often as I should've been to be a supportive as a father.

I continued to place the priority of the streets before my own children. There were times, though, when I thought I was doing something by giving them money here and there. But that was not what they really needed. More than anything else, they needed my *attention*, not my *money*.

Many fathers believe that as long as they provide the basic necessities for their child's survival, that's sufficient. They also have the misconception that as long as they pay child support, that's enough. But raising a child means more than providing food and shelter or paying the bills. It means providing emotional support, and above all, providing love.

The Truth is in the Youth

In the words of the old African proverb, "It takes a village to raise our children." But when the village is crazy, then it will produce crazy children. Dr. Jawanzaa Kunjufu concurs that young people have a story to tell, if only adults will listen.

When he asked teenagers, "What do your parents and teachers tell you about school?" they responded, "Get a good education and work." When he asked them how they felt about those comments, they answered, "Get a good education for what? Work hard for who?" They also want to know the relevance, the need, or the reason for each lesson.

Dr. Kunjufu believes that young African-Americans stopped asking questions and began cheating when they found out that the most important objective in school was not learning but receiving good grades. He further claims that our youth have determined that securing employment is based more on *who* you know rather than *what* you know.

According to Dr. Kunjufu, young African-Americans see numerous ways to make money without getting a good education or working hard. He also notes that young people will say, "I'm going to be like Michael Jordan, Allen Iverson, Jay-Z, or Beyonce," without an appreciation of what it requires to *become* anything. They are motivated to *be* great, but not motivated to *become* great, which requires discipline, sacrifice, time management, vision, patience, and above all else, work. He attributes this misconception to young people watching "instant success" stories on television, instead of observing how their parents earn a living.

Just like adults, children will encounter obstacles that seem to jump out of nowhere to block their paths. Help your children to understand that these roadblocks are a part of life and that they can be overcome.

Adults, too, need to learn this lesson. Everyone would succeed in every attempt and win every race if there were no obstacles. Your job is to be persistent and work through those obstacles. If you find only a few obstacles along the way, chances are you're not really challenging yourself. If you want to experience the feeling of sweet success, make your goal a challenging one!

Chapter 4
Shun Not
the Struggle

"It is not the light that we need, but fire, it is not the gentle shower, but thunder. We need the storm, the whirlwind, add the earthquake."

—Frederick Douglass

struggle - *verb*. to make great efforts, to labor hard, to strive, or contend forcibly under difficult conditions.

Rather than accepting my struggles as a necessary part of life, I tried to find the easy way out. In my early teens, I became a juvenile delinquent and was considered by many people as one who would never amount to much. My friend, Nate, and I used to smoke marijuana every day before we went to school. Nate's parents were marijuana dealers. We would go and steal a handful of marijuana from their supply and put it into sandwich bags. We would be so high in class that it was ridiculous. It didn't make sense how we wasted so much time getting high on superficial chemicals, rather than using that time in the quest for knowledge.

But smoking marijuana was not the biggest problem I was wrestling with. I was also stealing cars and hanging out on the street corners with my friends during school hours. Toward the end of my seventh-grade year at Calverton, I was arrested for breaking into the new condominiums being built not far from my neighborhood and was sent to the Charles Hickey Juvenile Detention Center. Since I was a juvenile, my parents were the only ones allowed to pick me up from the police station, and after that, I had to stay home until my trial date. However, my dad warned me that if I ever got into trouble again, he would not come down to get me. As my father would say, "Ba-ba-boy, if-if-if ya git locked up and go to jail, you will stay there — cause' I ain't coming to git ya!"

Did I believe him? No.

One day, while I was waiting for another trial date and skipping school, I was caught throwing rocks at cars coming down the highway, trying to make the cars crash into each other. A police officer spotted me and chased me into the alley until several police cars blocked me in and placed me under arrest. They called my parents, and my father told them that he was not coming to get me, so I was taken to the juvenile detention center. This time, my tenure at Charles Hickey lasted much of my seventh-grade school year. When I came out I was even more frustrated and furious. Rather than having learned to respect the law at Charles Hickey, I'd picked up from fellow inmates even more schemes for surviving life in the streets. I became even more devious and started getting into even more trouble.

Eighth grade came around, and after several suspensions, I was expelled from Calverton Middle School for fighting and was sent to Harlem Park Middle School. On the third day at my new school, I got into another fight because somebody got smart with a friend who lived around the corner from my house. Harlem Park Middle School didn't waste any time with me. I was immediately expelled. The school board ultimately sent me back to Lemmel Middle School, where I finally made it to the finish line: I graduated from eighth grade. I believe I graduated as a result of social promotion since I hadn't done much work.

Borrowing the Benz

My father was a working man. He never knew the sun, he worked so hard — he was up and working before it rose and was still breaking his back when it set. Because my father held two jobs, he wandered home at the end of each day drunk with exhaustion, desperately looking for somewhere to lie down. When his head finally hit some surface — a pillow, a couch cushion, or even the back of a chair — he said, "Good night" to the world and slept like the dead. You could hear him throughout the entire house, "Sn-nooock, cl-cl-cloookk . . . sn-nooock, cl-cl-cloookk." He couldn't help himself. He had sleep apnea, which temporarily stole his breath.

As he fought to sleep and breathe all at once, outside sat his brand-new, money-green, 1987, S-Class, Mercedes Benz.

Well, not exactly … he had an old, beat-up, '77 Chevy Impala, the color of peas, which I called a Mercedes Benz. It sat before our house many nights, unbothered, ignored, waiting for him to regain consciousness and come warm its seats in the early-morning hours. Until, of course, I discovered its worth.

In my sixteen-year-old confidence, I began "borrowing" the "Benz". I'd cruise the city for two or three hours at a time, with the seat leaned so far back that I could barely see the cars ahead of me, let alone the road. With the radio turned on "Deaf" and in the welcome company of my friends, I drove from one side of town to the next. I was a thief, but my antics could neither hurt nor worry my father — he was sleeping.

As soon as he stopped breathing, in-between his snores, I'd sneak up beside him, find his pants, reach down to the lint-filled bottom of his pocket, mute the keys resting there with my hand, and then flee. Before he resumed his snoring, I was tiptoeing out the front door, down the slick, marble steps, and into the front seat of his car.

When I returned from a trip, I simply parked the car in its original spot, sent the radio dial to its home (a gospel station), and restored the keys to his pants pocket. If another car had filled his parking space in my absence, I parked elsewhere and prayed for my father's forgetfulness. My prayers seldom went unanswered.

One particular night, when my buddy, Ron, and I went to see two girls living in East Baltimore, my usual course was disrupted. As we pulled out of the apartment complex's parking lot, I failed to notice a sign that read "No Left Turn." We were listening to a rap song and doing just as it suggested, "diggin' the scene with our gansta' lean." Our front seats were reclined back nearly onto the back seats. It didn't matter that I couldn't see a thing around me — I was impressing the girls as we were leaving.

The dial on the dashboard clock read nearly 4:00 A.M. I was tired and dreading the rush back into town — I had to make it home, snuggle the "Benz" back into her parking space, fold the keys back into my father's pants pocket, and climb between my own sheets before he awoke.

As I made the illegal left turn, I neither saw nor heard the approaching police car's siren. I noticed not one flash of red light, not one burst of blue. My seat was too far back to catch a glimpse of anything through the rearview mirror, and the radio was blasting too loudly to even hear anything else. As soon as I turned, the police car crashed into my dad's '77 Chevy Impala.

The police car had disassembled and was completely wrecked, but because of its hard, steel frame, my dad's car stood strong. Aside from the collapse of the front windshield, driver's side doors, and the bumper hanging somewhere to the side, it remained intact.

The police officer jumped out of his ruined car and ran toward me with a slew of rhetorical questions and with one arm waving in fury, all before Ron or I could exit from our daze.

"Didn't you see me coming? Didn't you hear my siren? And what are you doing making a left turn here, anyway?"

Before one word of explanation escaped my mouth, he was on the radio calling for backup.

Inside my head, I said a thousand prayers, *Lord, I won't ever take the car again. I won't even get in it with Dad driving.*

I won't curse no more, Lord. I won't cut school. I won't fight with my little sister. I won't daydream in church.

Realizing that my prayers would be useless, I decided I'd better play hurt. Maybe, if my father walked into an emergency room and saw me hanging on to just a thread of life, he might pity me rather than kill me.

The back-up police officers and paramedics arrived, and I pretended to be half-dead. All of a sudden, my eyes were rolled into the back of my head, my feet were tossed inside the dashboard, my body was twisted and pulsating, and my lifeless arm lay contorted in the backseat.

As the paramedics carried me away on a stretcher and hoisted me into the back of the ambulance, I was still hoping for a bit of mercy. A police officer asked for my father's phone number, so that he could have him meet us at the hospital. Not three seconds after I recited it, I had a seizure. I convulsed on that gurney like a newly captured fish, screaming, "Somebody help me! I can't breathe!"

The paramedic closest to me bent down and whispered in my ear, "Boy, shut up. Ain't a darn thing wrong with you."

I ignored that. He was hindering my plan.

"Somebody help me, please!"

At the hospital, a team of doctors rushed over to me. "What's the problem?" they asked. But to answer them too clearly wouldn't save me from Dennie Miller. I acted as if I was drifting in and out of consciousness.

"Where does it hurt?" they persisted.

"Everywhere! Ouch! I'm having a seizure! I'm dying! Somebody! Anybody! Help me!"

78

By now, the doctors were all well aware of the non life-threatening injuries I proclaimed to have, and began laughing at me. And before I had said anywhere near the number of prayers I needed, my dad came marching down the emergency-room hallway with my uncle at his side.

I heard their voices and feigned death. When they were beside me, I peeked through my half-closed eyelids to see my father's face. I searched for pity, but found none there.

At moments like this, when my father couldn't contain his emotions, he stuttered beyond comprehension. He couldn't capture and drag one word from his mouth right then. All his feelings ran together in a train of broken syllables, "G-g-g-g-got, ah, ah, g-got, g-got, darn, m-mmmum, mack, Macka mmma, ki, ki, kkkk." He would sigh, "Phew!" take a breath, and start back up again. "Ki-, ki-, kill, kill, kill, ki-, ki-, kill, kill, kill, kill ya. Got darn, Michael, I'm gonna kill ya!"

The doctors raced to stop him from wrapping his hands around my neck. While he breathed, and before he began another round of stuttering, I interrupted him.

"Dad, Dad, listen to me! I got about a thousand dollars in my jacket at the house. I was saving up to buy a car. Please, take as much money as you need. Fix the car. Take all of it, if you have to. Please, Dad!"

Between his bouts of stuttering, and his gasps for breath, his mind registered what I'd said. At once, his chest settled back into place. The last words he spoke were as clear as water, "Well, I'll see you when you get home."

Once again, I had survived.

High School High Jinks

After I graduated from middle school, I went to Carver Vocational-Technical High School, where I continued my disruptive classroom behavior. By this point, many people had given up on me; likewise, I had given up on myself. I didn't desire to change my behavior, nor did I think I *could* change my behavior. So, when I arrived at Carver High School, my pattern of behavior followed me. During ninth grade, I felt a little pressure to fit in with the socially-cool kids, so I continued my delinquent behavior. But at the same time, I discovered a reason to suppress my hyperactive and disruptive behavior — girls.

Although I somehow managed to complete ninth grade, I got expelled in tenth grade for my disruptive behavior. The school administrators had a policy that if a student was suspended three times in one year, he or she had to be expelled from the school. As usual, I felt compelled to test the waters. When I was facing my second suspension, I was told that I couldn't come back to school unless I brought a parent back to school with me. I didn't want my parents to find out that I was in trouble again, so I paid my friend's uncle ten dollars to pretend to be my dad. I knew that he was an alcoholic, but I didn't know he was going to come to the school drunk. I said to myself, as I sat in what was supposed to be the parent conference with the principal and this drunk, *Michael, what in the world have you gotten yourself into now?*

The principal, whom the students called, "Wonder Woman" because of her resemblance, grew suspicious because my so-called Dad smelled like liquor. She had enough sense to know that my mom was a well-respected Christian woman who always wanted to know what was going on with her son. Later that afternoon, Principal Wonder Woman called my mom and asked her if my dad had visited the school earlier that day. When my mom told her that he had not, Principal Wonder Woman became fed up with me and expelled me from Carver High School.

I was devastated because graduating from Carver High School was a tradition of the Miller family. All of my brothers and sisters had graduated from Carver, and I was in line to be the eighth person to graduate. As a result of my expulsion, I became very distraught. I begged and pleaded for Principal Wonder Woman's mercy not to expel me. Putting my pride aside, I told her that I would be on my very best behavior from that point on, and that I would do what I was supposed to do. I promised to not run in the hallways, cut class, crack jokes, or be a class clown, but I had cried wolf so many times that she didn't take me seriously. I couldn't persuade her that if I wasn't given the opportunity to stay at Carver High School, my disruptive behavior would get worse than it was before. She didn't understand that at Carver, I had something to aspire to, a reason to want to graduate that had nothing to do with myself or my future. I couldn't get my family to understand my point, either. They said that Carver was just another school. Nobody understood that if I couldn't go to Carver, I had no motive for finishing school.

For many years, I harbored a lot of anger and bitterness toward Carver High School and its principal for expelling me. My perception was not that I had placed this burden on myself;

instead, I embraced anger, bitterness, and hostility toward learning. My Carver High School experience became another race in my life that I didn't finish.

The Breaking Point

I fully understood that I was disruptive in class, and that it was wrong to bring that drunk to school. I knew I was a class clown and that I was wrong for running down the hallways, but now, all I wanted was a chance. I knew how bad my life would become if I didn't get that chance. I was heading toward delinquency, and being expelled from Carver High School was the breaking point.

I ended up at Walbrook Senior High School as a consequence of being expelled from Carver. This was the high-school version of the notoriously violent Lemmel Middle School. My conduct became even worse than it had been at any other school. I still chose to hang out with the wrong crowd, and I never went to class. I had plenty of opportunities to get into trouble, and I took advantage of every one of them.

At the time, Walbrook High School was being renovated. To accommodate all of its students during this process, Walbrook merged with another high school, Southwestern High, for three years. This merger brought on tensions between the schools and made it difficult for the administration to keep up with all the students. Each school started and ended its school day at a different time. Because the teachers couldn't keep up with both school's bell schedules, more students cut classes, roamed the halls without passes, got into fights, and left school early.

Within a year, I had become completely discouraged. I had no motivation to finish school and no aspiration to succeed. The streets were calling me — and I answered.

I became a typical, high-school dropout, spending most of my time trying to find a decent job that didn't require a high-school diploma. There *were no* decent job available. Not unless you didn't mind cleaning toilets. Looking at the other high-school dropouts in my community, I understood why people without an education were looked down upon. Many of them had ended up in jail, ended up on street corners selling drugs to escape a life of poverty and the unemployment line, or had been shot and killed. I could see no sign of hope that I could make it as a dropout, or that I could even survive. I didn't know of anyone with a high-school diploma who'd made it in Sandtown, either; much less had gone to college.

Are You a Thermostat or a Thermometer?

One of the reasons that I dropped out of school was because I could not handle the pressure. When pressure came my way, I didn't know how to adjust to the obstacles and adversities in my life. Likewise, there is a pivotal difference between a thermostat and a thermometer. A thermometer reflects its environment. It simply shows what the temperature is. It doesn't change anything in its environment. It just registers the rising or falling of the temperature. It exerts no influence on what is around it; rather it's influenced by its environment.

A thermostat is different. It measures the temperature and then responds. If the temperature is too high, a thermostat may shut off the heat. If the temperature is too low, a thermostat may trigger the heat to turn on. It measures temperature *and* it does something about it. Just as a thermostat registers its surroundings and changes them when needed, we should not simply "rise" and "fall" in response to problems and difficulties in our lives. We should not passively allow harmful situations to happen, feeling as if we have no power.

We should become more like thermostats, motivated by difficulty and adjusting to change. You should believe that something can be done; a solution can be found; a hurt can be healed.

Advice columnist Ann Landers once said, "If I were asked to give what I consider the single most useful bit of advice for all humanity, it would be this: Expect trouble as an inevitable part of life. When it comes, hold your head high, look it squarely in the eye, and say, 'I will be bigger than you. You cannot defeat me.'" In other words, respond courageously and creatively.

I think I can! I think I can!

A great running back in the NFL is judged not by how many yards he runs in a season, but by how many yards he can run after his initial contact with the opposing team. In your race in life, expect to struggle at times. It is not the struggle that you will face that really matters, however, it is how you deal with the struggle that makes all the difference. Nothing worthwhile is easy. Frederick Douglass once said, "If there is no struggle, there is no progress." In order to progress in life, we must struggle at times.

The story of the butterfly clearly illustrates the necessity of struggle:

A man found a cocoon of a butterfly. One day a small opening appeared. He sat and watched the butterfly for several hours. It struggled to force its body through that little hole. Then it seemed to stop making any progress. It appeared as if it had gotten as far as it could, and it could go no farther.

So the man decided to help the butterfly. He took a pair of scissors and snipped off the remaining bit of the cocoon. The butterfly then emerged easily, but it had a swollen body and small, shriveled wings. He continued to watch the butterfly. He expected that, at any moment, the wings would enlarge and the body would contract. Neither happened!

In fact, the butterfly spent the rest of its life crawling around with a swollen body and shriveled wings. It was never able to fly. The man had acted with well-intentioned kindness, but he didn't understand the consequences. The restricting cocoon, and the struggle required to get through the tiny opening, were nature's way of forcing fluid from the body of the butterfly, as it achieved its freedom from the cocoon. Sometimes struggles are exactly what we need in our life. If we were to go through life without any obstacles, it would cripple us. We would not be as strong as we could have been, and we could never fly.

The next time you're faced with an obstacle, a challenge, or a problem, remember the butterfly. Struggle a little and then fly! Stay focused on the finish line. And while you are on your way there — *Shun not the struggle!*

Chapter 5
No Free Rides:
Life as a High School Dropout

"Every time I come in the kitchen, you in the kitchen. In the godd@mn refrigerator. Eatin' up all the food. All the chitlins. All the pig's feet. All the collard greens. All the hog maws. I wanna eat them chitlins. I like pig's feet! — I want you to get you're a_ _ up today, go out and look for a job! The word today is —*job. J-o-b!* You hear me?"
                              —Mr. Jones, *Friday*

free ride - *noun. slang.* something that can be acquired without the usual effort or cost.

My father made it clear that there were no free rides in his household. Anything I wanted, I had to work hard for it. Plain and simple.

He would blatantly say, "Boy, if you are not in school, you will get a job and work. And if you don't, you will git da hell out of here!"

When I first dropped out of school at the age of sixteen, I thought that I was on top of the world. I had the mentality of a superstar, and I was certain that I was special. I felt safe on the streets, confident that my street-smarts would enable me to handle any situation that might arise.

My dad requested that the grown children who lived in his household pay him twenty dollars per week to cover rent, food, utilities, and telephone. Instead of paying the money, I always griped about how much my dad would make if all his children paid him twenty dollars every week. I didn't realize that my dad was trying to instill accountability, responsibility, and the art of living on a budget within us. By requiring us to pay bills that we would have been paying anyway, had we lived out on our own, he was giving us a taste of what adult life would be like once we finally did leave home.

Even though twenty dollars is only a small percentage of the cost of running a household, I thought it was too much money, so I decided to take my dad's advice to those who wouldn't abide by his rules: Move out. "If ya don't like it, you can ge-ge-ge-ge-get out!" he would say. "Shoot, I pa-pa-pay da bills around dis here house. If you don't like my rules, g-g-g-go — and, ah, rah, get your own place a-a-and ah, ah, m-m-make, make (pause) make your own damn rules."

So that's what I did. I was eighteen years old, and, at least in my own eyes, officially a man. I moved out of my parent's house with hardly a stable income.

I found an inexpensive apartment for two-hundred-eighty dollars a month. Although it was two-hundred dollars more than I was used to paying, I thought I could afford it. The only things that I moved into my new apartment were my clothes and a set of clean sheets. I didn't even have a bed. Because I couldn't afford a mattress I had to improvise, so I put my clothes under the sheets and slept on them. Food was another problem. I quickly realized that my parents weren't cooking for me anymore and that I didn't know how to cook, so I ordered pizza and Chinese food.

With my newly acquired apartment came newly acquired bills, and with those new bills, my funds quickly got low. After paying the bills, not including the rent itself, I had little or no money left over to buy food. I felt homeless in my new home because I was hungry all the time. But I couldn't bring myself to move back home. My image was more important than eating or keeping warm. Meanwhile, my money continued to get low from trying to be "Mr. Big Shot." By this time, I was filled with too much pride to ask for any type of assistance from anyone. *I'm grown now*, I thought, *I gotta find my own way.* So, I took the now-and-later approach to survival. I would eat a meal now and save the leftovers for later. I would preserve this food in the refrigerator to eat throughout the week until it was empty again. Or I would stop by my parents' house to say hello and sneak in a free meal. I would grab a few extra pieces of chicken and some biscuits at dinner, and then I was ready to go home. That was my weekly routine, especially on Sundays.

Meanwhile, my house was void of furniture and life. Sometimes, the only edible items in my refrigerator were lard and water. No one knew about my poverty — because of my pride. I pretended that my apartment was fully furnished and that I had my finances under control. During the second month, I finally managed to buy a bed by postponing payment on my rent. By the third month, I could buy a living room set and a television. I figured that my apartment was presentable enough to invite my new girlfriend Nikki over to see how I was living. In the meantime, rent was still due. I hadn't paid rent since I'd started living there and that had been three months ago, and the unpaid bills were piling up.

I purposely procrastinated on paying my bills so that I could furnish my apartment to look presentable for guests. My goal was to build a cozy ambience. My best friend Ron, the same friend who was with me in the car accident with the police officer, soon moved in with me. His girlfriend's frequent visits turned into frequent sleepovers. She ended up moving in. I was trying to help my buddy Ron and his girlfriend, and I barely had the means to take care of myself.

Not surprisingly, I got evicted. One morning, after living in my first apartment for just four months, I received an unexpected visit from the rent-court constable, accompanied by the maintenance men who came to set my belongings outside. He knocked on the door and asked me if I could pay the past due rent to avoid eviction for nonpayment. I told him that I could go and get it. He shook his head and said, "No, sir, we don't have time for that. If you can't give the property manager the total balance due immediately, we're going to have to evict you from this apartment."

My pride immediately disintegrated. Frantic and desperate, I begged and pleaded, "Sir, please, I can go get the money right now. You see, I planned on paying it, but I never had a chance to make it to the rental office. I was going to make the payment the other day, but the rental office was closed."

The rental office was right next door to my apartment. He knew that I was lying and continued to shake his head 'No'. Desperate, I continued my already failing negotiations, "As a matter of fact, now that I think about it, I paid the rent the other day." My story was too inconsistent and unbelievable, and I knew that he knew I was telling a flat-out lie. It was too late. The maintenance men whizzed past me, scooped up all of my belongings, and set them out on the street. I felt humiliated with everything I owned sitting on the curb, and thoroughly ashamed that I had let my financial responsibilities get out of control. Even the girl next door who'd had a crush on me witnessed my eviction. Figuring that I had nothing to lose, I asked her for her phone number.

"Oh, no!" she replied emphatically, "You must be trippin'! I don't want a man who's broke and can't pay his bills!"

So there I was on the curb with my cozy apartment furniture. My apartment was in a rural neighborhood, so I had to walk about a mile to use the pay phone to call my dad to come and get me. By the time I walked back to my belongings, just about everything was gone except for my pillow. I couldn't believe that people would come by and steal my belongings. By then, I was like a dog on a fire hydrant — I was pissed off!

Being on my own meant that I had to accept my responsibilities. After this episode, I realized that I wasn't as ready for those responsibilities as I had thought. I thought I was a man because I was living on my own, but I still had the mentality of a boy. I failed to realize that being a man meant not only *having* responsibilities, but also *taking care of* them. Just because I was legally old enough to live on my own, didn't mean that I was mature enough to do so.

Most importantly, I realized as I sat on the curb with my few remaining possessions, while the rest of my belongings were scattered across the city, that my possessions didn't make me a man. I realized that spending the past four months trying to furnish an apartment rather than paying my bills was a poor choice. My freedom, too, had been stolen. The only difference was that I had stolen my freedom from myself by being irresponsible.

Life is all about choices, and my choices had taken me right back to where I'd started, to the place that I had tried so desperately to escape from — the place that I had called home for most of the eighteen years of my life. I went back to Riggs Avenue.

How Ya' Living?

I must admit that I was one who felt like I didn't deserve to live at all. After I dropped out of school, I hung out on the streets every day, doing nothing to better myself. I tried to find various jobs, but nothing stuck. I also dealt with a secret that I had never confessed to anyone, not even to God, Himself. I could barely read. And although God knew my shameful secret, I didn't talk to Him about it. I tried to suppress it into the darkness of my soul, thinking that one day it wouldn't matter. It only later came back to haunt me — all of the days in school when I was being a class clown, cutting class, skipping school, and not reading regularly.

Because of my illiteracy, I didn't even know how to fill out a job application. When they asked my sex on an application, I would write in "Every day."

Are You Living or Alive?

During my life as a high school dropout, I was alive but not living. And there is a fundamental difference between living and being alive (and between dying and being dead, for that matter). Living is doing more than what needs to be done, and being alive is doing just enough to get by. Most people, it seems, do just enough to keep themselves alive but not enough to *live*. They don't start living until they receive some drastic wake-up call. Those who don't need such a call experience many more happy years than the average person.

Often, it's not what somebody else is doing to us, rather, it is what we're doing to ourselves, which is causing our depression. It saddens me to know that many African-American teenagers, especially boys, are addicted to marijuana and other drugs or involved in gang violence. I can definitely relate to that. Unfortunately, these boys think, just as I did, that manhood is not about building a future, but about how much time they can do in jail. Many young people, including so-called men over eighteen, think that manhood is about how many babies they can make who they're not going to raise. Many of them think that real men call their women b_tches, whores, sluts, and tricks. Well, silly rabbit, tricks are for kids! And if you dare to call a woman a b_tch, which is a female dog, and you were born from the womb of a woman, what does that make you? The answer: A puppy. Better yet, that would make you a "Son-of-a b_tch."

Conversely, many women declare, "All men are dogs." But the Bible tells us that man was created in the image of God. How can women state that all men are dogs when at the same time you declare that man was created in the image of God? By doing so, you're not just rejecting men, you are, subconsciously, rejecting God. Likewise, if you believe that all men are dogs and continue to date this type of man, that makes you just what he's calling you — a b_tch — because you are subconsciously being the female dog that he proclaims you to be. Sisters, do not continue to buy music by men who insult and degrade women. Thus, these men are getting *rich* by calling you a *b_tch*.

Many of us are suffering from what I call, "Unconscious, low self-esteem." Although we may not be conscious of this low self-esteem, we may be subconsciously exhibiting low self-esteem. Because we think poorly of ourselves, we sit back and wait for the pleasures of life to fall into our laps. To rise above this mentality takes *faith* and *fortitude*. It takes *grit* and *grace*. It takes *Divine* help and *human* determination.

Are You Living for the Weekend?

Many people are more concerned with finding thrills than fulfilling their purpose in life. The Reverend Al Sharpton once said, "Anytime you just live from thrill to thrill, you have reduced yourself from a child of God to some freak of the Devil." Now all the Devil has to do is thrill you, and you go for the next thrill. The musical group, Farrar, once wrote a song entitled, "We're living for the weekend". But how can you live for the weekend, when most of the week is not the weekend? Do you think that five days of each week are nothing, which means that most of your life is an irrelevant waste of time? But if you've been reduced to a freak of the Devil, whatever and whoever *thrills* you *controls* you.

And it isn't just thrill-seekers who allow themselves to be controlled. I always wanted to control myself, but with my lack of education, I was being controlled by the system. I was controlled by where I lived. When I was incarcerated as a juvenile, I was controlled by what times I was allowed to eat, sleep, or watch TV. I've heard people say things like, "They are trying to move Black people to the suburbs." If you're on welfare, others *can* dictate where you live. But if you take charge of your own life, the system can't dictate where you live.

Above all, I've learned a lesson that I will never forget: In life, there are no free rides. You must develop a strong work ethic.

No More Pain

My childhood was marked by my father's absence. Our family's livelihood depended on him, and his determination to sustain us pushed him to work constantly. It was this very determination which prevented him from spending quality time with me or any of his children. For this reason, I yearned for his retirement. I viewed his work schedule as an impossible obstacle — as long as my father worked, I would never truly know him. With his retirement, I could begin to learn his ways, his thoughts, and his dreams. I could begin to feel like his son.

With just a year of work to go, I could hardly contain my excitement. Finally — we would converse. We would laugh until our stomachs ached. We would hang out and share meals. We would make up for a lifetime of emptiness. In twelve months, I would say "Daddy" and truly understand what it meant to be loved by the man named Daddy.

Three months into my father's final year of work, with just nine months before the forging of our new relationship, he succumbed to kidney failure. I'd lost him just prior to his retirement, and he'd never known the feeling of a workless day. Suddenly, this honorable man, well-respected in our home and community, was taken. A cold day in March 1996 left me distraught and with the distinct feeling that I would travel life's difficult journey alone.

A few months after my father's death, I was the same man — unemployed and uneducated, yet his physical absence complicated things further, and I was near desperation. At twenty-five, I was tired. My life had been a series of disappointments and misfortunes. I could barely see myself through, let alone view life optimistically. My pitfalls had overwhelmed me, and in a single, bleak moment I felt no hope. I wanted to banish all the pain and sorrow; I wanted to wash away the unbearable hurt over my father's death. I could not conceptualize tomorrow.

I asked myself, *Why keep running just to come in last place, anyway? Why pretend that things would get better? Why should I even try?* With nothing left to hold onto, I gave up. Out of the darkness and desolation of my soul, I cried out for death as a comforter. I decided to commit suicide and put an end to it all.

I called a hospital inquiring about the number of pills necessary to induce suicide. Thinking she was answering a hypothetical question, the nurse on the other end asked, "How much has the person taken? And what kind of medication is it?"

I answered, "A half bottle of Tylenol."

The woman, either unaware or unconcerned that I was asking for myself, told me, "If a person takes at least a bottle, I suggest that you take them to the emergency room."

Determined to end my pain forever, I took two large bottles of extra-strength Tylenol. It was around 11:00 P.M. on a summer night. After ingesting the pills, I drove away from downtown Baltimore with no destination in mind. After an hour, I started to feel very dizzy and sick to my stomach. I pulled the car into a high-school parking lot, thinking I could recuperate from the nausea. I don't remember much after that. My only memory is falling down in the school's football field. Somehow, I'd walked to the field's center and collapsed. I laid there, in the darkness, for an hour or more.

Sometime before I'd submitted completely to the pills, a friend of mine, Tim, noticed my parked car. Tim, a minister, didn't usually hang around the heart of the ghetto, but for some reason, he was there. After searching the neighborhood

97

extensively, he was compelled to walk through the football field. Pitch black, the field offered no light by which to see, but Tim, sightless, trekked through it. Eventually, he noticed that I was collapsed in the middle of the dark football field.

I vaguely remember Tim's voice in my ear saying, "Mike, Mike, hang in there, buddy." I also remember him making an earnest petition and crying out to God — "Father, I stretch out my hands to thee. There is no other help that I know!" Ironically, these were the same words my mother used when she was fed up and didn't know what else to do with me. Immediately following Tim's plea, I passed out. I fell into a deep sleep that promised to rescue me from all of the pain. I just knew that peace was coming, that I was through with my sorrow forever.

And then, suddenly, I was in an emergency room with tubes shoved down my throat and a hospital staff working frantically to pump from me as many pills as they could. Despite the choking sensation inspired by the tubes, I cursed and hollered. The gagging reflex didn't prevent me from expressing the anger over my rescue — I let the doctors and nurses know they weren't saving a grateful man. Once the staff had done all they could, they gave me some thick syrup to soak up the remainder of the medicine in my system. This syrup was the worst thing I'd ever tasted. It was thick and black, with a chalky taste, but I was forced to tolerate it. I wanted so much to go back to sleep, this time forever, but no one would allow my departure.

I was anxious to leave the hospital to try again, because my plan had been mysteriously thwarted, and this time I was going to try the surest way out.

"No, Mr. Miller. You can't leave here right now. We have to make sure that you're safe," one of the doctors said.

"Ah, no, the hell y'all won't!" I replied. "I'm getting the hell up out of here! You can't tell me what to do. I'm a grown man! You must be out of your d@mn mind, doc!" I didn't care about my safety. I wanted to be free of my pain.

I tried to leave the hospital, but the doctors screamed out, "Security!" The next thing I knew, I was upstairs in the Cuckoo for Coco Puffs ward.

Didn't they get the picture? Couldn't they see that I was tired of running my race? It didn't matter to me then that it was only by the Grace of God that I'd survived the suicide attempt. I just wanted to be free of my pain. I wanted to forfeit the race. Within the doors of the psychiatric ward, my spirit died. I fell down — way down — without a single thought of getting back up again.

Part 2
.....But We Get Up!

"Every morning in Africa, a gazelle wakes up. It knows it must outrun the fastest lion or it will be killed. Every morning in Africa, a lion wakes up. It knows it must run faster than the slowest gazelle, or it will starve. It doesn't matter whether you're a lion or a gazelle-when the sun comes up, you'd better be running!"

-Dr. Calvin Mackie

Chapter 6
Get Back Up Again!:
Looking Back to Move Forward

"Proverbs 24:16 says: *A just man falls seven times, but rises back up again.* Now what makes him just? Most of us in the church would call him wicked if he falls seven times. So what makes him just from the Bible's standpoint? It's that he has enough sense to rise back up. And not only get back up, but get back in line."

--Donnie McClurkin

to get up - *verb*. to rise to ones feet from a fall.

As weak and exhausted as I was, I summoned the courage to get back in the race. Over time, my anklebones strengthened, my legs fortified, and my heart filled with life. For the first time in twenty-five years, I stood on my own two feet. Sure, I was unsteady at first, but hope rushed and grabbed me by one arm; faith took me by the other, and perseverance said, "Follow me." I put one foot forward and said, "This step is for the baggage I've been carrying — all the hurt, pain, anguish, guilt, and turmoil I've suffered." I took a second step, and said, "This is for all the anger and animosity I've carried against everyone, including God." The third step felt best because it represented my failure as a father. "This," I said "is for the parent I've never been."

In Search of My Son

At this point, I realized that I needed to be a real man and be a father to my son. All the pain, misery, worries, doubts, setbacks, and obstacles I had faced (and would continue to face) were nothing more than speed bumps devised to slow me down long enough to teach me some lessons. Once I'd crossed them, and heeded their message, I'd accelerate again toward my ultimate destination.

I knew that God had a purpose for my life after I had miraculously survived my suicide attempt. So, I asked God to give me a chance to right my wrongs. I promised Him, if granted just one opportunity, I would do everything humanly possible to straighten my crooked path. With that covenant, God and I worked together to transform my life. Before I could consider moving very far forward, though, I had to take an anguished look into my past. I had to retrace my footsteps and find my lost sheep — my son.

The word *Sankofa*, which comes from the Akan people

of Ghana, West Africa, is derived from the words *san* (return), *ko* (go), and *fa* ("look," "seek," and "take," respectively). Translated, it means, "to move forward, one must return to the past." The concept is often symbolized by a bird flying forward with its head turned backward.

Sankofa helped me recognize the importance of self-evaluation and resolving past hurts to determine my future. At age twenty-five, I realized that it was time to retrace my footsteps and mend the relationship with my son. Finding him would be no easy task since Dévon and his mother had been missing from my life for nearly six years. Though I pretended not to have a conscience, I did. I'd simply chosen to ignore it. While in middle school, I had been told by Candy's foster sister that Candy had lost all of her children as a result of her drug abuse, but I never paid it much attention.

Surprisingly, after all those years of neglect, I actually found him. After calling a few places, then searching out his mother's family, and calling a few government agencies, I found out that my son was in the custody of the Department of Social Services. But I had to put up a fight before I could see him.

Man on a Mission

When I went to the Department of Social Services, I was informed that my parental rights had been terminated.

"How can that be?" I asked.

"Your son is about to be adopted by his foster parents. I guess that it's too late to be a father now, Mr. Miller."

I knew that I couldn't take no for an answer. Something crazy had to be done. Just like everything else in life, "All things are possible for those who believe." Even if no one had done it before, I was going to take care of my son. I asked the social worker, "Ma'am, is it possible for me to get my parental rights back?"

She replied, "Well, Mr. Miller, at this stage, it's very difficult for that to happen."

"But is it possible?" I persisted.

"Why are you trying to interrupt something that's going along just fine?" she asked.

My response was, "Because I'm on a mission!"

When someone's parental rights have been terminated, it's usually definitive. Most parents give up and stop fighting the system. It's a long, hard, tedious battle. But I was on a mission. All I wanted to know was if it was possible. That's it.

The social worker said sarcastically, "Mr. Miller, it will take a miracle,"

I smiled and said, "That's all I need to know!"

"But we're about to go through the final stages of adoption," she reminded me. She continued to try to break my persistent spirit by telling me about all the petitions that I would have to file. Subsequently, I would have to show just cause why I had not been in the picture until now. Then the judge would have to award me custody if he felt that I had grounds for reinstating my parental rights.

"Mr. Miller, do you have an attorney?" she asked.

"No," I replied. "My mother told me that God is a lawyer in the court room. I'll just represent myself. I've got Jesus, and that's enough!"

The social worker continued her sarcastic remarks and questions, all with the intent to deter my destination, "Do you have a job and a home in your name that would provide suitable living conditions for a child? You will have to meet the requirements of the home inspector. How are you providing for yourself? Do you know how to care for a child? What is your show-cause reason why your rights should be reinstated? Where were you the last six to eight years of his life? Right now, Mr. Miller, it's you against the Department of Social Services, because we're not recommending that your rights be reinstated. I just don't see it happening. Now, what is your response to that?"

Got Faith!

I was silent. I didn't have a response to give to her, because I couldn't fulfill any of the qualifications which she was stating.

"Yeah, that's what I thought," she replied. Then her voice got louder and she said, "You're just a typical Black man with an excuse. So, Mr. Miller, what do you have, then? You don't have a home. You don't have a lawyer. You don't have a show-cause reason for the judge to reinstate your parental rights. You can't even tell me where you've been for the last six to eight years of your son's life. Well, it's too late now. So, what do you have?"

I looked her straight in the eyes, as I yelled out, loud and clear, "Faith!"

Everything became silent. She was stunned by my humble yet arrogant response. Instantly, she backed away from me and sat down.

I continued to look deeply into her eyes to let her know that I was going to fight. Even if it meant going against the entire Department of Social Services, even if it meant putting my life on the line, even if it meant losing everything, I was going to fight. I was on a mission! I left her office without another word spoken.

Although I had faith, I needed God to show up immediately and give me directions. Things weren't looking very good for me, but for some strange reason, I still had faith. And belief or faith is the conduit through which God does the impossible.

I knew that my mission as a father was to reclaim that which I'd lost — my son. And I was not going to stop until my mission was complete. Even though the Department of Social Services had cast me out, I would continue to walk by faith and not by sight. I found great comfort and inspiration in knowing that the Bible declares, *"The steps of a good man are ordered by God, and he delights in his way. Though he falls, he shall not be utterly cast down."* –Psalms 37: 23–24.

Regardless of everything that the social worker said, I had received my orders to fulfill my mission. And what a lonely mission it was. I went back and forth to court, trying to file the petition to regain my parental rights. If it wasn't one thing, it was another. Either the weather caused the courts to close down, or one of the other attorneys wouldn't show up. Then there were postponements due to the judge's crowded docket, thus postponing the case until further notice. It was always something. I went back and forth to the petition hearing nine different times before the case was finally heard.

I didn't need a lawyer. Just like my mom, I walked in with favor and faith, and I represented myself.

All Things Are Possible!

Dr. Benjamin Elijah Mays once gave the charge to the Morehouse College graduating class of 1961 and said, "May you forever stand for something noble and high. Let no man dismiss you with a wave of the hand or a shrug of the shoulder." I tried to uphold those words. I was adamant that I would not let anyone "dismiss me with a wave of the hand or a shrug of the shoulder." I was determined to be heard.

The Department of Social Services' attorney and my son's attorney were representing the best interest of the child; they were both contesting against me. Yet, I stood resolute. After a grueling battle, the judge awarded my parental rights back on the grounds that I had not been legally notified of their termination.

It's amazing how everything works together for those who believe. My mission was not over just yet — I still had to battle to get custody of my son — but in the meantime, I had visitation rights, and this decision put a screeching halt to the adoption proceedings. Although the Department of Social Services wanted my son to be adopted by the family he was living with, as long as I met the necessary requirements, they had to work out a plan for reunification with me.

Initially, I was only permitted to see Dévon for the minimum one-hour visitation that the law allowed. This was partly because I gave them such a headache every chance I could get. We constantly disagreed about the best interests of my son. They just wanted him to be adopted — and I wouldn't allow it. I was determined to gain custody of Dévon. Many times, things got so chaotic between us that our telephone conversations ended in heated arguments.

I refused to let them pass me by as just a typical Black man. I wanted to make sure that they did their job. One of the things that I've learned from dealing with the system is that if you let them run over you, they will. Some social workers genuinely have the children's best interests at heart, but many just seem to be lazy or they have too many cases to manage.

The court system was ardently opposed to letting a young Black man who hadn't been in the picture for a while raise his son. In fact, the court records show that I went to court forty-three times in reference to my son. Dévon was in the third grade by the time I was given a plan for reunification, and he had been in the foster-care system for three years. Although they made me jump through all kinds of hoops to get custody of him, I didn't falter. So, fathers, it's possible to win a court custody battle. You just have to be devoted, diligent, and very determined.

It's Never Too Late

Some people want to put restrictions on themselves according to their talent, intelligence, or experience. Others worry about their age. But with God, one person can always make a difference, regardless of his circumstances or situation.

And age means nothing to Him. You're never too old — or too young — to finish what you've started. I remember once asking a group of nontraditional college students what they planned to do after they graduated. One student said, "Well, Mr. Miller, I would love to go to medical school for eight years and become a doctor, but I'll be forty-two years old by the time I finish medical school."

My response was, "Regardless, in eight years you'll be forty-two, anyway. Why not be a doctor when that time comes?"

You must understand — "Change is inevitable, but growth is optional." — Change will happen regardless, but you've got to choose to grow.

Begin Again

The time finally came for me to visit my son. We started out with one-hour visitations, with the social worker listening in on our conversations. Social Services thought that this arrangement would discourage me from visiting him, but it didn't. I'll never forget seeing him for the first time since he was an infant. As he walked toward me, he looked like an exact replica of me when I was a child. When he asked me, "Are you my daddy?" I responded by saying, "Yes, son, I'm your daddy."

I was trying really hard not to cry, but I began to break. I couldn't help but to release the emotion I had been holding back for so long. As we drew closer to each other, my heart began to beat really fast. Tears began to

111

pour down his face and he looked at me fearfully, as if he was afraid, afraid of being attached to his parents again — afraid of being left alone again. After all, he had been moving from one foster home to the next. And, at that time, I was a stranger to him.

I kept reassuring him that it was okay. As we hugged each other during this emotional moment, I began to feel what he was going through. He squeezed me tightly, as if he was desperately in need of a father to hug, to hold, and to cherish. It felt like a hug that had been backed up for so many years. I wasn't used to hugging with my parents, my friends, or my brothers and sisters. I wasn't used to that kind of love and affection. Hugging my son for the first time felt so good! It felt warm; it felt charming; it felt sincere; it felt genuine, and it made me feel needed as a father.

Escaping with Excuses

While we were hugging and embracing each other, I whispered in his ear something that I should have said a long time before. I said to him, with emotion, "I'm sorry. I'm so very sorry, Dévon. It wasn't my fault."

All he could do was cry his heart out, "Daddy, where were you?" He kept asking questions that I was not prepared to answer, "Daddy, where were you when they came to get me? What took you so long to come see me? Why weren't you there when I needed a father?"

I began to make up what I thought were legitimate excuses for my absence. I told him that I didn't know where he and his mom were when they moved. However, that wasn't what my eight-year-old son wanted or needed to hear. The truth was, if I had wanted to, I probably could have found him.

Not once during the conversation did I take the blame for what had happened. Not once did I take the blame for my faults. Not once did I admit to my eight-year-old son that I had partly caused the pain he was feeling or explain why I had not been there to catch him when he was falling. I didn't have any answers, only excuses. He didn't want to hear excuses. He wanted the truth so that true healing could begin.

We can't help or heal with lies. Dévon wanted to stop feeling the pain of not having his parents there when he needed them. He wanted the same thing that all other kids want: He wanted to call someone 'Mama' or 'Daddy', regardless of what his mother had done. What about Daddy? It didn't matter that they had moved. The years of my son crying himself to sleep was nobody's fault but mine.

Why, Daddy? Why?

As I stood there, while he was crying, I began to realize that he was feeling much as I had when I was his age, but in a different context. My father lived with me, but he stayed busy most of the time and was unable to give me his earnest attention. Now Dévon cried out for attention, just as I once had, "Why, Daddy? Why?"

When Dévon asked, "Daddy, where were you?" or "Why, Daddy? Why?" I threw a barrage of excuses in my son's face that were intended to make him feel sorry for me. But Dévon, even as a child, could cut through all that nonsense. For every excuse that I made, Dévon came back with a corresponding challenge.

I said to him, "I didn't know where you were. Your mother had moved and it was hard to find you."

And Dévon responded, "But why, Daddy? Why couldn't you find me?"

When I said, "I never had a father figure to teach me how to be a father," he responded with his continued tears and the repeated question of, "But why, Daddy? Why?" He wasn't fooled by my attempts to blame others for my failures.

Is It Too Late?

As he walked away, I just stood there, feeling puzzled. Things had started off okay, with tears of joy, but had ended with tears of pain and many unanswered questions. I left the building trying to figure out what had happened. I found myself upset, angry, and filled with rage. But with whom? God. This time I didn't curse Him out, though. I felt betrayed by God, as if He had turned His back on me. What ever happened to, "I will never leave you, nor forsake you?" I felt like God had set me up for failure, only to be rejected by my own son. I was being obedient to His great commission to go back and reclaim my son, only to find myself rejected. There I was, in the middle of downtown fussing God out, saying, "You set me up."

People were walking by me and saying, "He must be crazy!"

I began to get discouraged. Voices were beginning to

go through my head, saying, "Michael, you might as well give up. You can't fix a relationship that has already been broken. It's too late!"

Seeking for the Solution

The race of life is tough. You either get distracted or discouraged. You begin to doubt what you're doing and to question yourself. You've stumbled and been knocked down, but winners get back up and keep going. Just as Aaliyah suggested, we must dust ourselves off and try again. And that's exactly what I did.

I walked through the streets of downtown Baltimore, trying to find a solution to this madness. Everyone else was at fault, but not Michael. As I was walking along, I heard the lyrics to a Michael Jackson song on the radio, "I'm talking 'bout the Man in the Mirror/ I'm asking him to change his ways/ And no message could have been any clearer/ If you wanna make the world a better place/ take a look at yourself and make that change!"

The Apology and the Promise

As I listened, it occurred to me that I had to look at myself and admit my own wrongdoings. Therefore, I decided to use the lyrics from the song to take a look at myself and make that change! During the next visit, a week later, I made sure that my approach was much different. As soon as I walked into the visitation room, I told him very genuinely and affectionately, "Son, I understand what you're going through. It wasn't your fault. It was mine. I'm very sorry that you had to go through what you went through alone. I'm sorry that I wasn't there to hug and kiss you every night and tell you that Daddy loves you. I apologize for making partying and the streets a priority over my own son! If I could turn back the hands of time, son, I would, but I can't. Starting right now, I promise to always be there when you need me. But most of all, I will love you unconditionally, Dévon."

We cried together. All I could do was cry. That 'Thug Mentality' I thought I had went right out the window. I had finally reclaimed one of the most precious jewels in my life, my son. I had retraced and found my lost sheep. God had given me a second chance to right my wrongs.

That experience has taught me a valuable lesson: Honest and sincere apologies are the key to healing the pains of the past. I started doing what psychologists call introspection, or, self-examination, to try to find out where I had gone wrong. Self-examination is difficult for many of us because it compels us to do a critical analysis of *ourselves*, rather than of other people.

In order to acknowledge my faults, I had to start with the basics, such as apologizing and admitting my own faults and failures, rather than making excuses. In fact, the first step in any type of rehabilitation begins with either one of the Three 'A's. You must Accept, Acknowledge, or Admit that there is a problem. When you accept, acknowledge, or admit that you are partly to blame for your problems, you are on your way to solving them. Many people spend their entire lives playing the blame game, convinced that they are right all the time, rather than acknowledging the other person's feelings and views.

To stop playing the blame game, I had to acknowledge what I had done wrong, accept what I had lacked as a child, and admit that change had to start with me. Although I previously mentioned that I had never witnessed anyone in my community saying, "I was wrong", "I apologize", or, "I'm sorry", it was time for me to face up to my responsibilities and stop making excuses.

No More Excuses

Even though I had never imagined that God would make me work this hard to win back my son, it was time that I corrected my faults by standing up and being a man, a real man. All I had ever given my son was excuses. An old proverb says, "Excuses are like crutches; they're for the lame and the weak." If you continue to make excuses to your child, or for your condition, your life, or for neglecting your responsibilities, then you are either lame, weak, or both. It's a harsh statement, but it's true.

George Washington Carver once stated, "Ninety-nine percent of failures come from people who have the habit of making excuses." So many times, we have indoctrinated ourselves to blow balloons for our own pity parties. We pack our luggage to go on guilt trips. We even say that it's "The man" who's holding us down, when, in all reality, we're holding *ourselves* down. Many of us believe that if circumstances were different, we would be in a different predicament. Even if that's true, excuses are the language of failure. Blaming others means that you are not taking responsibility and ownership of your mistakes in your life.

117

This denial of ownership leads to a victim mentality and allows important opportunities to pass you by. It's easy to point the finger at everyone else's wrongdoings, but not our own. Remember — when you point a single finger at someone else, three fingers are pointing back at you!

Throughout my race in life, I would always blame others for my failures. I kept saying to my son, "I didn't know where you were! My father was never there to teach me how to be a father. I come from a community where I didn't see positive role models of fathers."

The truth is that I failed to look for my son and had resigned myself to not knowing where he was. I also used my background as an excuse for my failures. This was my crutch. Now let's be real. Racism is not responsible for African-Americans killing each other; *we are!* Growing up without a father in the house is not responsible for you being a deadbeat dad; *you are!* Your boyfriend or girlfriend is not getting on your nerves so badly that you have to go behind their back and cheat on them; *you want to!* You're not getting bad job reviews because your boss doesn't like you; *maybe you're lazy!* You didn't get a failing grade in class because your teacher had something against you; *you didn't do your work!* Nobody else is responsible for your failure; *it's you; it's you; it's you; it's you!*

We Fall Down, But We Get Up!

Throughout this entire ordeal, I kept reminding myself of the lyrics to the song by Donnie McClurkin, *"We fall down, but we get up! For a saint is just a sinner who fell down, and got up!"*

On your way to reaching your destination, you're going to stumble and take a few falls. When that happens, you've got to have the fervor and fortitude to get back up again, dust yourself off, and get going.

I've learned that as long as you lie down and remain stretched out, *passive and inactive*, you'll always make excuses for your failures. And as long as you keep talking about how bad things are, you'll never go anywhere, and you'll never do anything.

Even if you are down, you don't have to stay there and adjust. If I were to step in front of you and knock you off your feet, that's on *me*. But if you're still lying there the following week, that's on *you*. Though you may not be responsible for being down, you're still responsible for getting back on your feet. If ever you should fall down, make sure that you fall on your back, because if you can look up, then you can get up!

Yes, life is hard. Yes, life may tear you down and knock you down. In fact, life may knock you to your knees. But as I've found out, that's a good praying position!

Your condition is not your conclusion. Your current status does not dictate where you can go. It doesn't matter what you've been through, you can always fix what has been broken. No matter how many times you've fallen before, "GET BACK UP, AGAIN!"

Stop living in the past and put the past where it should be, behind you. It was only meant to propel you into the promise of your future. Your past should be a reference point, *not* a residence. We can become so overwhelmed by failures and mistakes that we just stop running, letting past failure

119

paralyze present opportunities.

If you want things to get better in your life, you have to rise and stand up to the situation! You have to rise above your obstacles so you can say, "I can be knocked down, but I will not be knocked out."

When you choose to lie down, it will *sap* your strength, but standing up will *give* you strength. When you lie down, it will *take* your courage, but standing up will *give* you courage. When you lie down, you'll wear other people out, but standing up, you'll just *wear out*. So stop lying down and waiting around for somebody to do something for you. Take charge of your life and — *Get back up again!*

Chapter 7
Begin with the End in Mind:
The Art of the Start

"The journey of a thousand miles begins with a single step."

—Lao Tzu

"You don't have to be great to get started, but you have to get started to be great."

—Les Brown

begin - *verb.* to take the first step in doing; to start.

end - *noun.* something toward which one strives; a goal.

mind - *noun.* focus of thought; attention.

Everything is possible once the runners have settled into the starting blocks for the race. As the starter judge announces, "Runners, take your mark! . . . get set! . . ." within a microsecond later, the runners brace themselves to burst out of the blocks. When the starter's pistol cracks, the

121

sprinters vault forward, expecting a win. But before they reach the finish line, they may fall, tear a muscle, or simply lose focus. Some may not finish at all. The race of life can be just as difficult, disappointing, and disturbing at times.

Focus on Finishing

You need to run the race of life with the finish line clearly in mind. Remember, it doesn't matter where you start; what counts is where you decide to finish. If we want to be successful in life, we need to determine what our long-term goals are. It is not how good you look in the starting blocks; rather, it is whether you make it across the finish line.

My life's race began to take on new meaning, and I began to be motivated to do something better for myself. I got tired of just being alive; I wanted to live. It was time to deal with the other ghosts that continued to haunt me — my education.

Meanwhile, I was still fighting for full custody of my son. If I wanted to present a better case to get custody of him, I would have to go back to school to get my GED. Earlier, I had tried seven times, but I didn't have any aspiration to succeed. So I dabbled in different GED programs, only to pay the fee and quit after a few days. As soon as I became distressed about not knowing how to do the work, I would just give up. The smallest things would turn me off and trigger me not to go back to GED classes. For instances, if I didn't like the way the teacher looked at me, got smart with me, or if I wasn't pleased with the time of day the class was held, I would quit. I wasn't motivated to get my GED, at all, because I had neither the inspiration nor the aspiration to get it.

But this time — I had a goal: I wanted full custody of Dévon. Also, the GED Program at Baltimore City Community College was different from the others I had attended. Finally, there was one GED program that could hold my attention long enough for me to graduate and finish my high-school education. The school provided weekly presentations on various topics by staff members. Visitors from both the financial-aid office and the admissions office also spoke to the students to motivate us to attend college after we received our diplomas.

I was twenty-five years old when I decided to attend class at BCCC, in search of hope, inspiration, and motivation to get me to the next level of my life. I was tired of having the windows of opportunity slammed close on me because of my lack of enthusiasm; I was tired of limited employment opportunities.

At first it appeared that I would have to wait to enroll. My entry scores were very low, which placed me in the Adult Basic Education (ABE) courses. Even though I'd had trouble filling out job application forms, I was shocked when the test administrator told me that my reading skills were on a third-grade level. I thought they were okay, even though most of my school time had been spent playing around and disrupting the class. However, it was not just a test to see if I could read the words. It was also a test to see if I could *understand* what I'd been reading. Unfortunately, this score meant that, technically, I couldn't enroll in a thirty-day GED class. I would have to finish the six-month ABE courses first. Then I would be tested

123

again. If I my literacy skills were high enough, I would be able to enroll in a GED course. Not wanting to wait six more months, I went to the program director, Mrs. Arah, and pleaded with her to let me into the GED program instead. She finally gave me the okay to take a GED class. However, she had several stipulations: I had to promise to attend class every day, to do all the home assignments that were required of me, and to behave like a mature adult in class.

GED classes were a new experience for me. When I arrived at my first class, I was very nervous, because I hadn't been inside a classroom for nine years. Even though I'd made a promise to Mrs. Arah about my conduct in class, I immediately regressed to my schoolboy ways of joking around, just as I'd done in high school. But the personality types were different from those I remembered. The typical students always talked about how they had been "A" students until twelfth grade. Others had been out of school for many years and now had children who had already graduated from high school. Still others were sick and tired of being unable to land a decent job to take care of their families. Then there were those, like me, who didn't initially take their education seriously, and, consequently, became disruptive during class time.

One of the teachers, Mr. White, stood out to me because he was young — in his mid-twenties, like me — energetic, and apparently understanding. Students often complained about not learning anything in the Language Writing class. So, Mr. White, who essentially taught math, decided that he was going to teach us both subjects to better prepare us for the exam. One week later, I came to class angry and upset because I was dealing with the frustration of my son's custody battle. During each lesson, I felt that Mr. White was picking on me for no reason at all. He would call on me, knowing that I didn't know the answers, and I would respond, "I don't know. You know, math just ain't my thang." When he called on me during the writing lesson, I felt that enough was enough. Then the question came that I didn't want to hear, "Mr. Miller, can you please read the passage?" Although it was just three paragraphs long, to a nonreader like myself, it appeared to stretch into three chapters. The students, who were in the same boat as I, all looked at me in anticipation of me reading the paragraphs.

As I sat there, knowing that I would be embarrassed by my reading skills, sweat began to pour down my face from my forehead. Would I pronounce the words correctly? Would I have to guess some of the words? Would I be stuttering while trying to figure it out? Other students began to mumble to themselves, "Man, I wish he'd hurry up and read. D@mn! It's not that difficult!"

Okay, Michael, I told myself, *you can do this!* As I began to read, I started to stumble and stutter over my words. My classmates began to chuckle out loud, as they had done when my third-grade teacher had embarrassed me in front of the class. Once again, the tables were turned on me, and I became frazzled and discombobulated.

Frustrated and angry, I jumped up in the middle of class and yelled, "I'm tired! I'm tired of this crap, and I don't have

125

time for this! I can't read! I can't write! And I sure as hell can't do math!" I slammed down the book and stormed out of the classroom.

The Turning Point

The teacher, Mr. White, followed me into the hallway, and, for the first time in my life, I started crying out of anger. I usually dealt with anger by keeping everything bottled up inside of me. I worried about other people's perceptions of my anger, as well as my beef with God and being angry with Him. Besides, I had tried voicing my opinion, and it didn't work. But that day, I had exploded with emotion.

Mr. White never asked me why I was crying. He just said, "You don't cry much, do you?"

"No, I ain't no punk," I said, wiping the tears from my face. "I don't cry. My eyes are just watery right now."

"Look," he said, "I don't know why you are crying, and I don't need to know why. But I can tell you this, if you apply that same energy from your anger and your tears toward your education, you will be very successful one day. I promise you."

That was the moment when I decided to take my education seriously, so that I could do better for myself and my son. Instantly, I felt like a new person. I was crazy enough to believe that if I said to a mountain, "Mountain, get out of my way!" it would move. My faith began to revive, and I began to feel good about the person I could become — a scholar — and not the person I was presently — a man without his GED who could barely read.

Unfortunately, many of us focus on who we are and not on what we can become. After that day, Mr. White made a personal commitment to work extra hours with me after class to help me meet my full potential.

A Promise to be Committed

Just as Mr. White made a commitment to work with me, I made a commitment to myself to finish what I'd started. Since I had been out of school for nine years, I would work extra hard to graduate. Determined to read and study for nine hours a day, I read everything I could get my hands on, including cooking directions, newspapers, candy wrappers, and soda labels. I carried a pocket dictionary with me wherever I went to look up unfamiliar words that I encountered. I made sacrifices for the betterment of my education, giving up television, giving up hanging out on the corners with my friends, and giving up going to parties all the time. It was time to stop playing games and deal with those demons that had haunted me for years. I thought that changing everything on the outside was the answer. But only when I started dealing with my fears, changing what was on the inside, could I get back into the race and finish everything that I had started. As Jose Villegas once said, "We watch what we eat, but never spend the time to find out what's eating us."

Whenever I did have time to watch TV, and a person said a word that I didn't recognize, I wrote down the word and looked it up in my pocket dictionary. By the end of the day, I would have about thirty or forty new words in my vocabulary. I did the same thing in Mr. White's class. I think he knew that I was writing down words, so he used unfamiliar words to challenge me and help me build my vocabulary. I was determined to get out of this rut. Because I was so dedicated and diligent with my education, I made significant improvements in all subject areas within three weeks.

Even though my in-class outburst was the beginning of my commitment to myself to take my education seriously, there were still times when I allowed doubt to set in. The closer I got to my goal, the more nervous I would become about finally finishing what I'd started to do back when I was in high school — to receive my high-school diploma. Just the thought of it would have my heart beating, and I would break out into a sweat. But in order to face the *demons* of my past, I had to *return* to the past.

When the time finally came for me to take the state GED examination, I had to force myself to leave my house to take the test. I've always been a person who feared rejection. In fact, this fear was one reason why I couldn't finish what I'd started. I didn't want to face the pressure of what might be or could be. I was afraid of failure. Many of us are scared to finish what we've started, because we fear what may happen if we don't succeed. I kept hearing voices of doubt telling me that if I didn't do well, I could lose everything — including my son — along with my hopes and dreams. I was scared of going back to my old way of living and barely getting by, but I also feared facing what it would take to complete this mission. The night before the exam, I couldn't sleep at all. I had to keep reminding myself why I was doing this, and who I was doing it for — my son.

If it is to Be, It's Up to Me!

I had relied on my mentor, Mrs. Arah, the program director, to get me this far. The only other constant motivation was my brother, Dennie, who was a mentor to me, as well. He consistently challenged me do to better with my education. He was always a prime example of a self-motivated individual by being an exemplary brother and mentor. Now it was up to me to use my internal motivation to motivate myself. I knew I had a lot on the line, so I kept repeating the slogan from a gold plaque on Mrs. Arah's desk, 'Just Do It'. I told myself, *Michael, if no one else is rooting for you, I am.* Now that I was pumped up and ready to just do it, I left my house to take my GED examination, but when I finally arrived at the testing site, my motivation went downhill. I was on an emotional roller coaster.

It was mid-October and the building was filled with a morning chill, yet I was sweating bullets. I contemplated quitting the race to avoid finishing what I'd started. I procrastinated from, *Just Do It* — to — *Just Do It Later.* Then I mentally compared the three people cheering me on with the many who weren't. I recalled the words which the Baltimore City Unit Chief of Social Workers had said to me, "Mr. Miller, there is no way that you will ever get your son again." Out of anger, I had cursed him out for getting smart with me. I played back the comment of the judge: "Mr. Miller, there is no way that you will be able to meet all these requirements in such a short time." My response to him was, "Go to hell!" I remembered the statistics on people of my economic and educational background, whose

129

chances of passing the GED exam in only five weeks were slim-to-none. I also thought about my so-called friends, who'd had the nerve to tell me that it was too late to even try to finish the daunting task of going back to school. My response was, "It's never too late!"

To motivate myself, I thought about the millions of African-Americans who had protested for their equal rights to receive an education in this country. They were spat on, beaten, and lynched, and had died to give me the right to drop out of school, live a meaningless life, and go back to school to take a GED exam. I said to myself, "I've got a right to be here!"

I thought about what seemed to be the only statistical data available about the survival chances of Black men, which served as a tool, rather, for them to lose hope within themselves: "By the age of twenty-five, the average Black man will be either dead, in prison, or under some type of police supervision, scrutiny, or surveillance." As I pondered those statistics and my actual age at that time, twenty-five, I said to myself proudly and boldly, "I must be a survivor!"

Yes, I realized that I hadn't had someone to nurture me and show me how to be a father, but I also thought about the great African-Americans who had made it in spite of all the obstacles they had to overcome. I thought about the number of Black fathers walking out on their families and running away from their responsibilities and the rarity of Black fathers actually stepping up to the plate. But I also thought about the untold stories of the Black slaves who had escaped slavery, migrated to the north, worked, and then gone back and bought freedom for

130

themselves, their wives, and their children. I thought about the stereotypes, the obstacles, and the perceptions by which modern society views African-American men. And, I remember saying to myself, *Today, I can help change the world's perception of Black men and Black fathers by finishing what I've started — my education.*

Due to my consistent positive self-talk, I empowered myself to take the GED exam. Motivating yourself with positive thoughts can make a difference in everything that you do. You need motivation all day, every day. As one motivational speaker once said, "People often say that motivation doesn't last. Well, neither does bathing. That's why we recommend it daily."

As soon as my thoughts finished wandering, the test administrator said to the classroom full of eager GED test takers, "Please put everything away except a pencil. The test is about to begin." The race was on. By the time I had finished taking the exam, there was no one left in the room but the test administrator and myself. When I left, I kept my head up. Even if I didn't pass, *I had finished what I'd started!*

The Big, Brown Envelope

Because I was the last person taking the exam, I was sure I had failed the test. I didn't want to wait for the test results to come back to tell me that I had failed all subjects. I wanted to stay focused, so I immediately re-enrolled in the GED program. One night my buddies, Jay and Sam, came over to my house to pick me up before we went to go partying to celebrate Jay's birthday. Though I was finished with partying, I thought it

131

was okay; it was my boy's birthday. Jay, who was always nosy, noticed the big, brown envelope on the kitchen table. "Mike, what's in the big brown envelope?" he asked. "Food stamps?"

I replied, "Nuttin'. Just some bad news about school, and I ain't got time to be hearing some bad news right now. I'm focused, my head is on straight, and I *will* get my G.E.D. — some day."

"Man!" Jay said. "Why don't you just give it a try? You don't even know what the results are."

"Obviously, you *don't* understand. Just an ounce of rejection will take me away from reaching my goal of receiving my GED. I'm on a mission."

"Oh, yeah? So that's the way it's going to be, huh?"

"Yep!" I replied.

"Well, let's see," Jay said.

"No, no, *no*!" I responded. "I don't want to know right now, man! I already know what it is, and I'm in my second class right now and preparing to take the exam again."

We started tussling over the envelope. Jay held me down while Sam grabbed it and read the results. Sam yelled out, "You passed! You passed! You passed! You've received your Maryland high-school diploma! Man, you got your GED!"

I stood there in shock from the news. Not only had I passed, but I also passed with extremely high scores. I was astonished and overjoyed. Once again I found myself in tears, breathless, and overcome with emotion. I had waited many years for this moment.

Other than the custody battle for my son, this was another reason for me to believe that I could do anything I wanted to do.

All I had to do was stay focused. Words can't express the elation I felt that night. I started thinking about all the obstacles that I still had to overcome in running my race. I pondered all the jobs that I still couldn't get. I remembered my mama kneeling at the foot of her bed to pray that one day all the madness in my life would end and I would get my act together. Tears poured from my eyes as I stood there thinking. The words of Mohammad Ali came into my mind, and, with my voice cracking, I shouted, "I am the greatest!"

We went out to celebrate Jay's birthday after my emotional episode, but, mentally, I wasn't there. I was still in my living room, hearing Sam tell me that I had received my Maryland high-school diploma. I couldn't wait to rush home to see and hold the high-school diploma with *my* name on it.

There was an elegant graduation celebration for all the students who had obtained their GED. My GED graduation was a grand occasion that made me feel extremely special. We all had caps and gowns. The men wore dark-colored shirts and ties, while the women were dressed in business suits, just like high-school graduates, only better. Our family members were there to cheer us on. I was even chosen to give a speech as the class representative.

Nontraditional graduations seem to be more emotional than traditional, high-school graduations for both the students and the guests. Although many traditional, high-school graduates have overcome obstacles to earn their diplomas, the nontraditional students have overcome major setbacks, disappointments, heartaches, pains, and struggles to go back to school and finish

133

what they'd started. The emotional triumph is unlike any other. There is nothing like the feeling of opening doors that were once slammed in your face, disproving your critics' claims that you will never make it, and beating the odds stacked against your success. Some students began to cry before they walked down the aisle, and they stopped to comfort and congratulate each other on a job well done. I heard many graduates say, "I can't believe I've done it!" Many guests, having lived through difficult experiences themselves, were also overwhelmed with emotion.

Immediately following the graduation, we had an elegant reception in the college's cafeteria organized by Mrs. Arah to reward our efforts. She had set up the reception room as if it were a banquet hall. There were elegant bouquets on every table, a jazz band playing while we ate with our families, and caterers wearing black suits and bow ties serving our food. It was one of the proudest days of my life.

Stick!

Although you set your goals, sometimes you may backslide into complacency or succumb to the temptation to quit or give up. Along with self-doubt, you will struggle with many distractions every day while you are striving to reach your goals, such as your family members, your surroundings, and your circumstances. The road to success is not just that. You just have to keep running to reach your goals in the midst of temptation.

During your race, you must keep your eyes on the prize. Great track coaches teach their runners to focus ahead at all times. If not, they will have a habit to become distracted and may lose focus. It is important to keep your eyes fixed on the finish line. This will prevent you from losing your stride and your momentum. As a point of reference, use the finish line as your goal.

The importance of keeping one's eyes ahead while running was powerfully illustrated during an attended track meet. There were four teams competing in the 440-yard relay race, the most highly anticipated race of the track meet. As the runners for each of the teams blasted out of their starting blocks, they collectively unleashed enough force to make a Lamborghini go from zero to sixty MPH. At top speed, their hands slashed through the air like switchblades. All four teams were neck and neck as they turned the corner for the home stretch. The winner of the relay race would be decide upon the performance of each team's anchorman. The anchorman for one of the teams mistakenly looked back. As a result, he messed up the timing of the third runner who was giving him the baton and caused a fumbled exchange.

The anchorman for the other team, though, kept his eyes on the finish line and began slowly building momentum. As he approached the anchorman, the runner of the third leg shouted, "Stick!" which is the call that occurs when the baton is exchanged. Once the third runner hollered "Stick!", this was the indication to the fourth runner to not look back, but just to stick his hand back and receive the baton. As a result of the flawless exchange of the baton, the third team won the race. The anchorman's ability to keep his eyes focused on what was before him was the key to their victory.

You cannot afford to look back. If so, you will fumble the baton and lose the race. You must have the *persistence* to go the *distance* in order to finish the race. The third runner is coming around the corner, and he/she is shouting to you "Stick!" When the baton is passed, will you finish the race? Will you give it all you've got? Will you have a strong finish?

Chapter 8
Overcoming the Hurdles:
A Setback is a Setup for a Comeback

"So many times, it happens too fast; you trade your passion for your glory. Don't lose your grip on the dreams of the past. You must fight just to keep them alive."

—"Eye of the Tiger", Survivor

hurdle - *noun*. an artificial barrier or obstacle, in which competitors must overcome or leap, in order to win the race.

We will all face our own unique set of hurdles in our lives. Just about all of us will trip over some of them before getting to the finish line. Many of us will get up and run again, eventually crossing the finish line victoriously; whereas, others will trip over the first hurdle

137

and never get back up again. Some will even use their precious time on the track to whine and complain about the fact that they've stumbled over the first hurdle, not understanding that the time clock of opportunity is still ticking. How do I know? Because this is the same thing I did when I was faced with a unique set of hurdles in my life.

Uh-Oh! Another Hurdle!

I now had to face a series of hurdles of trying to win custody of my son. First, the problem was my education, so I went back to school to get my GED and enrolled in college. Then the problem was that I hadn't taken any parenting classes, so I went to the Department of Social Services' Young Fathers/Responsible Fathers Program and finished with honors.

It was one roadblock after another. I would do everything they asked of me and more, and still they weren't satisfied. One day, I got so sick of the stupidity that I lost my cool and cursed out the judge, the social workers, and the supervisors. I didn't mean to curse them out. I was doing everything in my power to do what was required of me to gain custody of my son, and this still didn't matter. It was the only way that I knew to express my anger at that time. After that, they all said that it would be impossible for me to get my son back.

This was a Job for Superman!

I didn't know that a man would have to work so hard to gain the custody of his child. There are many cases when the mother could smoke crack and abandon the children in the house. The Department of Social Service would get involved, but the mother would be granted reunification with their children after completion of a thirty-day drug rehabilitation program. Having gone through my experience, I realized it was not that easy for fathers. I knew that the battle which I was fighting was bigger than I was, though. Who was I to fight an entire system? As the old saying goes, "It's not the size of the dog in the fight, but the size of the fight that's in the dog." They thought they were fighting against me, but they were really fighting against the God in me.

So, in times like these, I knew that this was a Job for Superman (God)! I knew that He was the only one who could come to my rescue immediately. As I struggled to get custody of my son, I was always walking by faith and not by sight, because the scene was too devastating to watch. But because I had faith, I knew that one day I would get him back, and I made sure that I always had the necessary living arrangements just in case.

I'll never forget what the social worker's supervisor told me after I'd cursed out the judge and the social workers. She took it very personally, "Mr. Miller," she said, "you will never get custody of your son. You bastard! I'll see to that. You will never get him. Not over my dead body."

I sarcastically replied, "Well, if I was you, I would check my insurance policy to make sure everything is okay, because you must be dying. Because I will get custody of my son! You just wait and see!"

After an emotionally taxing and grueling custody battle, I won against the entire Department of Social Service, as well as against the court system, with the help of God. Consequently, I was awarded full custody of my son. If I had relied on "reality" or what others perceived as possible, I would have failed long before.

The Next Hurdle — College

The next hurdle that I had to overcome was enrolling in college. Mrs. Arah and Mr. White continued to push me to go further with my education. After repeatedly hearing them tell me that they saw great potential in me, I finally decided to take their advice.

To reinforce her faith in me, Mrs. Arah offered me a full scholarship to attend classes at Baltimore City Community College. In the back of my mind, I said, "Nah, not right now. Maybe later." At that time, I was still equally scared of success and failure. Just like so many of us, I made excuses and procrastinated. After Mrs. Arah's constant advice to challenge myself and go beyond the GED, along with Mr. White's mentorship, I began to really believe that I could achieve my goal of becoming a college student and someday to graduate. Motivated by their insistence to move to the next level, I made the critical decision to attend college.

Mrs. Arah had an extra reinforcement which persuaded me to go to college. As always, every time I visited her office, I saw the gold plaque that read, 'Just Do It'. Had it been left up to me, I would've procrastinated further. However, the words on that plaque just kept ringing through my head. It's important, as you strive to reach your goals, to have some slogan to read constantly and remember during your times of weakness. Unfortunately, procrastination often sets in, and 'Just Do It' turns into *I'll Just Do It Later.*

There was another incident in particular which made me so determined to stay focused and finish my education. I will never forget the day that I first enrolled in college. I was discouraged about attending college because I had been out of school for nearly ten years. I kept thinking about how my skills would not be as sharp as the other students in school.

Mrs. Arah constantly reminded me, "Michael, you can do this! There is nothing different between them and you. As long as they put on their pants the same way you do, you can do anything that anyone else can." After constantly hearing this advice, I finally went to enroll in Baltimore City Community College. I intended to go to college for a semester to see if I liked it and if I would fit in. I was being very passive about my approach to this particular goal. Besides, not too long before, my only goal had been to get a GED to help me get a better job.

Now, I had gained confidence in myself and wanted to go to college to stay out of trouble and out of harm's way. Even though I had worked hard to earn my GED, I still battled with the everyday temptations of hanging on the corners. I still needed additional reinforcement once I started college. My grandmother always said that an idle mind is the devil's workshop. So, I had to stop being complacent. I had to be constantly moving, doing something productive with my life to ward off those thoughts of quitting what I'd started.

141

I decided to enroll in college only one month after receiving my GED. I was still so excited about having my GED that I started walking around telling people that I had my PHD: **P**ublic **H**igh school **D**iploma.

Many of my friends would walk up to me with jealousy in their hearts, saying, "Michael, it don't take all of that."

And I would arrogantly respond, "Yes, it does! If you had been through what I've been through, maybe you would be like this, too."

You should've seen me. I had a swagger in my walk. I strolled into college with my thug gear on, confident that I belonged there. My left shoulder was high and upright, my arm close to my side, while my right shoulder dangled downward, arm swinging. I was bopping my way into my destiny. When I arrived at the college, I met with my advisor to go over my academic goals and to pick my major. After our introductions, she went over my transcript and realized that I had just received my GED.

I explained that my intention was not to have a major, but to go to school so that I wouldn't be on the streets wasting my life away.

She asked me, "Mr. Miller, how many credits do you plan on taking this semester?"

"Well, that depends," I replied. "How many credits do I need to be considered a full-time student?"

She responded, "You must take at least twelve credits."

I immediately replied, "Twelve credit hours are exactly what I need. I need to stay busy. Can you please enroll me for twelve credit hours, ma'am?"

She shook her head. "Uh, uh, uh. I don't think so!"

Shocked, I replied, "Why not?"

"Well, I think that this is a bit too much for you, considering your educational background. Besides, you'll be in the classroom with high school graduates who are fresh out of school."

I pleaded with her to allow me to go to school full time. I began to quote my grandmother's saying, "Ma'am, you *must* understand: 'An idle mind is the devil's workshop,' and if I don't go to school full time, I may start something that I'll regret later. I can do this. Just give me a chance to prove myself. I've partied enough in my lifetime. Now I'm ready to be serious about my education." I wanted to make sure that the devil would no longer consider my mind as a place to set up shop.

She said, "Mr. Miller, I understand what you're trying to do. But right now, we have to look at what's realistic."

I said, "Realistic, my a_ _! Ma'am, I'm on a mission!"

"Now, wait a minute, Mr. Miller. First of all, you need to watch your mouth."

I replied, "Okay, I'm sorry!"

But then she said in a condescending tone, "Mr. Miller, I don't think that you should go to school full time. After all, you only have a GED, and you just got that!"

I angrily replied, "Ah, no, the *hell* you didn't! What do you mean, I *only* have a GED?"

Because I lacked a college-level vocabulary, I cursed her out thoroughly to show her exactly how I felt about her comment and the *way* she had delivered her words. I remember thinking, *It's one thing for someone to try to bring you down when you're not doing the right thing, but it's a crying shame to bring you down when you're trying to live right.* She was trying to downplay my hard-earned accomplishment, as if getting a GED was not of great significance. She was also implying that a GED, unlike graduating from high school, was not an academic honor.

After all my attempts to change her mind, her perception of how she thought I would do in school never changed. She insisted that she wouldn't recommend my entering college full time. It didn't matter to me whether I passed or failed. I knew I would have to live with the outcome. But after I caused chaos in her office, she told me that she didn't think I had the right attitude to do well in college. As I walked out of her office, she said, "A college is not a place for thugs like you. You ought to be thankful that you finally got your high school diploma! Go get a job somewhere!"

As a result of her condescension, sarcasm, and lack of understanding, I decided not to enroll in college. I walked away from her office as angry as I had been when I made the outburst in Mr. White's class. Only this time, there was no one there to calm me down and tell me that everything was going to be okay.

I realized that out of all of the condescending things that this advisor had said to me, she was right about one thing: I had only *just* earned my GED. I came to her office with enthusiasm — only to leave with anger. As I left the building, I downplayed the situation to myself, *College ain't for everybody, anyway.* All because of what someone said to me, I left the school knowing that it was back to the street corners. How could she disparage something that I'd worked so hard for? How could she steal the joy that I felt before I had walked into her office?

Who's Stealing Your Joy?

The answer is that my advisor stole my joy and disparaged my accomplishments because I let her do that. No one can do anything to you unless you *let* them do it to you. If people who are, themselves, regressing see that you are making progress, they may try to stop you because they don't want to see anyone doing better than they are. If you give them the power to hold you back, either physically or mentally, your lack of progress is not their fault but actually your own fault for handing that power over to them. No one controls *Your* destiny except *You*.

Nothing can be stolen unless you leave yourself vulnerable for a thief to rob you of your goods, your joy. Did you leave the front door unlocked or give your house keys to someone who can't be trusted? Was the back door unlocked? Did you put your keys underneath the doormat, thinking that a thief wouldn't check to see if someone was stupid enough to put them there? Have you put your faith in man and not in God? A thief always scopes out the scenery first, and if he feels that a house is worth robbing, he will steal all your hard-earned money and possessions — and your joy.

Because I had let someone steal my joy, I decided not to enroll in college, and I went back to a wasteful life of doing nothing. Two months went by, and the first week of the semester was approaching. In desperate need of one of her pick-me-up hugs,

145

I stopped by Mrs. Arah's office to say hello. Her hugs made me feel wanted and appreciated, like a son being hugged by his mother.

After another one of her huge, affectionate hugs, she asked me, "Michael, are you ready for school next week?"

My response was, "Well, there's been a slight change of plans. Instead of following the advice on your desk that says 'Just Do It', I've decided to wait and just do it later."

I explained to Mrs. Arah about my encounter with the advisor and how she'd made me feel with her comment about my GED. I then told her about how she thought that the minimum twelve credits might be too much for a former GED student. I also explained how belittled her comments had made me feel while I was in her office.

"What?" she responded. "You go back to school to register, and you tell her that you have the right to take as many credits as you want to take!"

Taking her advice, I went back to school the following day to pay the same advisor another visit in her office. While I was waiting for the advisor to come and meet me, I started mapping out the schedule of courses I wanted to take.

Can a Rose Grow Out of Concrete?

Not only did I take Mrs. Arah's advice, I also took the advice from the words of Tupac Shakur. In an interview on television, he stated:

"If you walked by a street and you were walking on concrete and you saw a rose growing from concrete, even if it had messed up petals and it was a little to the side, you would marvel at just seeing a rose grow through concrete. So why is it that when you see some ghetto kid grow out of the dirtiest circumstance and he can talk and he can sit across the room and make you cry, make you laugh, all you can talk about is my dirty rose, my dirty stems and how I'm leaning crooked to the side, you can't even see that I've come up from out of that."

I was now prepared to go back and reclaim my joy. Once I was in the advisor's office again, I asked her, "Ma'am, can a rose grow out of concrete?"

She said, "Huh?"

"Please answer the question," I said. "Is it possible for something as precious as a rose to grow out of something so hard as concrete?"

Her response was, "Well, young man, it appears to me that it's not likely for a rose to grow out of concrete."

My response was, "I thought that would be your answer." I just knew that she would reject this analogy, just as she had rejected the idea that a young, Black man, such as myself, could defy the odds and be a worthwhile person one day. If you believe that a rose can't grow out of concrete, chances are you believe that a glass is half empty and not half full.

Mrs. Arah had already informed me that I didn't have to agree with the advisor's recommendation regarding college; her recommendation was just that, only a recommendation. So, I arrogantly told her, "Ma'am, *this* rose, which has grown from concrete, would like to enroll for eighteen credits. These are the courses that I would like to take for this semester."

She looked at me and realized she had no choice but to sign my registration slip, even though she thought I was making a mistake.

After she signed the slip, I grabbed it from her desk. As she grunted to herself and squirmed in her chair, I kindly said to her, "Ma'am, a rose *can* grow from concrete. God may allow rain to come and penetrate the concrete. And once the concrete has been pounded, the water will be absorbed. And then the hard concrete must return to its original state of sand and cement dust, making it easier for the rose to grow, just as easy as it would be to grow in dirt."

She just stared at me with this puzzled look, as if I was crazy, and as if to ask, "What scholar did he get that from?"

So I answered her without even being asked, "Oh, by the way, I got that information from a scholar named Tupac Shakur."

As I walked out of her office and went to the registrar's office to get my printed schedule, I realized that the incident had been a blessing, not a curse. Because of her initial rejection, I ended up taking eighteen credit hours instead of twelve for my first semester in college. I also made up my mind that I would never give someone that much power over me again. I don't ever plan on relinquishing my power without a fight. Whatever or whoever is stealing your joy and power, take it back!

Shake it Off!

I soon became the focus of the media's attention as they followed my progress, but I was distraught by the headlines which read: 'Michael Miller: Student Bites Off More Than He Can Chew'.

It was tough to endure all the media criticism of my decision to take eighteen credit hours. The media critics started to pull out statistics to prove that the course load would be too arduous for me. However, the criticism just fueled my drive to excel even more.

I finished that semester with a 4.0 GPA. I wasn't satisfied with using only my first semester to prove that my critics and the advisor had been wrong, so I decided to enroll for fourteen credit hours during the summer, twenty-four credit hours during the fall semester, and twenty-one credit hours for the final (spring) semester, and all this while working full-time and being a single parent.

That experience has taught me that I could receive victory in the midst of adversity. This lesson is also clearly illustrated in the story of "The Dog In The Well":

There once was a farmer whose dog fell into a dry well. After assessing the situation, the farmer sympathized with the dog but decided that neither the dog nor the well was worth the trouble of saving. Instead, he planned to bury the dog in the well. When the farmer started shoveling dirt into the well, initially the dog panicked. But then it dawned on the dog that every time a shovelful of dirt landed on his back, he could shake it off and step up on the rising level of dirt. As shovelful after shovelful fell on him, the dog said repeatedly to encourage himself, "Shake it off and step up! Shake it off and step up!" Soon, the battered and exhausted dog stepped triumphantly out of the well to safety. What he had at first thought would bury him, had benefited him — all because of the *way he handled* his adversity.

You Feel Me?

We've all heard, over and over, the common phrase, "You just have to be motivated to reach your goals." That's easy for people to say when they're already motivated. But what do you say to motivate people who don't see their purpose in life and *can't* seem to get self-motivated? What do you say to a young man or woman who feels as if there is no reason for living? What do you say to someone who feels as if they don't have a purpose? We obviously can't keep using the same approach. It is apparent that this old and tired advice is not working. Usually, we argue with them and tell them that they just have to find their purpose and get motivated somehow. This is our typical response, but it's also the wrong response. It will only make them more distant from you, because they will feel that you don't understand their situation.

"You just have to be motivated," will appear to be a meaningless answer because it's not always that obvious. If they do not receive helpful advice when they come to us for answers, they will turn to someone who will understand them. Their outlets will eventually be their friends out on the street corners, maybe drugs, alcohol, prostitution, or even violence.

To guide these seemingly lost souls, you must give suggestions that will help them easily understand you. In fact, the most important component in counseling is the psychology of understanding. Young people want to be understood, and not told how to feel or why they need to stop wasting their lives.

We should not disregard what young people are saying simply because we can't understand them initially. We should ask them to clarify the meaning behind their statements, so that we can properly advise them and guide them to success.

Once we begin to interpret what they are saying rather than criticizing them for using street slang, we will find out that they experience the same things that we do, and that it is possible to understand, relate to, and guide them using our own experiences and our wisdom.

For example, when young people say things like, "Do you feel me?", or, "I can feel that," and, "I'm not feeling this person," what they really mean is, "Do you understand me?", or, "I understand that," and, "I don't understand/agree with this person." These phrases refer to the idea of someone being felt or touched metaphysically, not physically.

Keys to Motivation

To inspire our youth to be motivated, we must give them the formula for motivation, which is Aspiration + Inspiration = Motivation. Therefore, in order to be self-motivated, you must first have aspirations. Your aspirations are your goals and your reasons to be motivated. When someone or something gave me a good reason to be motivated, it became a lot easier to reach my goals. You have to have something to aspire to and know the reason why. My reason for being motivated was my son; I wanted to provide something better for him. Even when I felt like giving up on my son, the reason why I was doing it outweighed my negative thoughts. At first my life's purpose was very foggy, until I realized what my aspirations were. Things are much clearer for me — now that I've got my aspirations in order.

Second, you must have inspirations. Someone or something must inspire you to be great. Daily inspirations are important to become motivated or even to stay motivated. After my graduation, I posted copies of my GED diploma throughout my apartment — in the bedroom, the living room, the closet, and in the bathroom — to remind myself where I had come from and where I was going.

Don't wait for an award ceremony, promotion, friend, or mentor to show appreciation for your work. Take pride in your own efforts on a daily basis. Give praise to yourself. Continue to overcome your hurdles and keep the end result in sight. Always see the big picture of the ultimate goal you are working toward and the benefits that will come with it. These keys to motivation will help to overcome the hurdles in your life.

Whenever athletes run the hurdles, they face many obstacles which could cause them to stumble. But the goal is still the finish line, and the focus is on winning the race. The hurdles are simply obstacles to overcome. Those of us who are not athletes will face hurdles in our race, too — obstacles which can trip us up or slow us down in the pursuit of our goals. Though we may fall, we must keep in mind that these hurdles are nothing but *setbacks* that are *setups* for a *comeback*.

Chapter 9
A Leap of Faith

"There is an air of expectancy at Morehouse College. It's expected that the student who enters here will do well. It's also expected that once a man bears the insignia of a Morehouse graduate, he will do exceptionally well. We expect nothing less . . . ."

—"The Charge of the Graduating Class of 1961"
Dr. Benjamin E. Mays, President, 1940–1967

leap of faith - *noun*. the act or an instance of believing or trusting in something intangible or incapable of being proved

Soren Kierkegaard, a Danish Christian philosopher, argued that a significant, religious-belief system should not be based on physical evidence. Instead, meaningful religion requires what he called "A leap of faith," which requires complete trust in God. Kierkegaard's point is that any logical system contains gaps that can only be bridged by a leap of faith, the absolute uncertainty of truth in the absence of evidence. Since faith can neither be proven nor disproved, a leap of faith is undertaken in a state that Kierkegaard calls, "Fear and trembling".

At some point, you will reach a stage where there aren't any rational reasons for making a move. You have to make it without any logical excuses. You have to take "A leap of faith."

I decided to take my leap of faith during the Blizzard of 2000. Logically, it wouldn't make sense to leave Baltimore and drive through a deadly blizzard, with twenty-eight inches of snow predicted. It didn't make sense to leave home, but sometimes logic doesn't make sense. I was bold, confident, and willing to take this leap of faith.

On several occasions, Mrs. Arah proclaimed that I should go to Morehouse College in Atlanta. At that time, the only colleges that I was familiar with were local colleges in Baltimore. I wasn't sure what school I wanted to initially go to. I didn't know about colleges out of state, no less Morehouse College. But I knew that I no longer wanted to go to school in Baltimore because of the distractions from my friends and the temptations of the streets, so I aggressively pursued colleges outside of Maryland.

By this time, I had scholarship offers from more than twenty-five schools. Eventually I narrowed down my choices to Yale, Duke, Johns Hopkins, and Florida State University, all whom offered me some type of scholarship.

But Morehouse College had not responded to my application. The only thing I had received was a postcard stating that they had received my application. They didn't seem to care about all the national publicity from magazine covers, the front page of *Black Issues in Higher Education*, a listing in *Who's Who among Students America*, the U.S Dept of Education accolades, or my GPA. Morehouse was determined to make me wait. To them, I was just another student who was desperately trying to get in.

Go to "Da House"

I was getting fed up with waiting to hear from Morehouse College, so when an inner voice told me to drive to Morehouse College, in Atlanta, Georgia, I immediately called up my buddy, Ron and told him of my plans. As products of West Baltimore, we had never traveled physically or even mentally beyond the Beltway (Interstate 695), much less outside the state. But something kept pulling at me, telling me that I needed to go. Although there were severe snowstorm warnings along the entire East Coast, I didn't change my plans. I remember asking myself, "Do I turn back now?" and replying, "No." Without hesitation I gassed up the Camry, and we headed for Atlanta, seven hundred miles away — in the middle of a snowstorm. It was 10:00 in the evening and snow had begun to fall. I picked up Ron and my Aunt Dot, who kept us entertained during the trip. Once she knew I was going to Atlanta, she asked me to drop her off at my dad's hometown in Bertie County, North Carolina. That was a big mistake. She was supposed to show me how to get there, but she was too intoxicated.

I didn't know anything about the interstates or the highways. All I had ever known was Baltimore City. By 10:20 P.M., we were

155

on our way to Atlanta. As we got to the tip of Virginia, more snow began to fall, but we kept on driving. Although Ron didn't have a driver's license, I asked him to drive half the distance to Atlanta.

We were planning to be there in twelve hours, by 10:00 the next morning. As Ron was driving my car, the police pulled him over and asked him for his license and registration. I became very nervous and said softly, "Yo, what are we going to do?" He didn't respond. Instead, he gave the police officer his brother's driver license information.

Meanwhile, my aunt was in the backseat, cursing out the police officer, calling him all kinds of names. He asked us to get out of the car, and she continued to curse him.

I said, "Aunt Dot, will you please be quiet? You promised me that if I let you come, you would behave!"

The policeman warned her that if she said anything else, he would lock her up. Instantly she sobered up.

Just when the police were ready to let us go, they began to get a little suspicious about Ron's driver's license story. Before I knew it, they were taking Ron off to jail to officially check his identity.

Again, I asked myself, *Do I turn back now?*

No, I thought, so I proceeded as planned.

In the meantime, I was relying on my intoxicated aunt to give me directions to Bertie County, but she was too drunk to remember. I could barely see through the snowy gusts, but I drove around for about three hours before I knew exactly where to go. By that time she was asleep. I continued to drive through that freezing blizzard with no heater. I could barely see, as the snowfall began to get even heavier.

I finally reached Bertie County. After dropping off Aunt Dot, I had to drive all the way across North Carolina to get back to Interstate 95. My heels were freezing, because air was blowing in through the bottom of the driver's side, dented door. I was scared, all by my lonesome, and I felt like turning back. Instead, I humbled my spirit and asked God to be with me on this journey.

Running On Empty

Fourteen hours had gone by, and I was still driving through the gusty winds of the blizzard. But I had to stay focused, because my exit, Interstate 85, was soon approaching. When I reached South Carolina, I needed some more gas, so I left Interstate 85 at the next exit and turned onto a dirt road. The gas station was several miles down the road. It was an old, storefront gas station, much different from the ones I was used to seeing in Baltimore.

Four White men were standing on the front porch of the service station. One was a deputy sheriff, who was chewing tobacco with a straw in his mouth. After I finished pumping the gas, I politely asked the men, "Excuse me. Can you please tell me how I can get back on 85 going to Atlanta, Georgia?" They didn't respond. They just looked at me with funny expressions on their faces.

Now, I was really pissed off because I knew they'd heard my question. But they continued to ignore me, so I repeated very loudly and clearly, "Excuse me. Can you guys tell me–?" Before I could finish, the deputy sheriff responded, "Goddamn it, you in da wrong town, boy. You in da wrong town."

I was scared as hell! They must have been the Ku Klux Klan. Maybe they were still upset with Kweisi Mfume for causing all that ruckus about the Confederate flag. I got in my car and hauled tail on what I hoped was the way back to Interstate 85. Somehow — I made it.

Georgia on My Mind

I finally arrived in Atlanta around 2:30 in the afternoon. A drive that would usually take about eleven to twelve hours had taken me twenty hours, thanks to the blizzard and getting lost. Although I was exhausted, I felt like Fanny Lou Hammer, who once said, "I'm sick and tired of being sick and tired, but I am in no way tired." At least there was no snow in Atlanta.

When I got to Morehouse College, I was overcome with emotion by the statue of Morehouse alumnus, Martin Luther King Jr. in front of the chapel.

I also saw something that I'd never seen in my life: African-American men wearing business suits with crispy-clean dress shirts, neckties or bow ties, and polished dress shoes. They were sharp!

Where I come from, African-American men seldom stand around together unless they're on a corner selling drugs. And even when I did see them together in the 'hood or at a club, they weren't wearing suits. After that inspirational moment, I knew that it was really time for me to pursue a college education.

I made my way to the admissions office to talk to Dean Sterling Hudson. My childhood neighbor, Mr. Al, always told me, "Whenever you do business, never talk to rookies. Always deal with the big man." Dean Hudson's assistant informed me that I needed an appointment to see him. She insisted that he had a very busy schedule and wasn't seeing anyone. However, after that long ride, and as determined as I was, I wasn't going to take "No" for an answer.

No matter how much she kept telling me I couldn't see the Dean, I kept insisting that I needed to see him. I began telling her that it would only take a minute.

Before I knew it, a tall, intimidating-looking man came out of his office and said, "What seems to be the problem here, young man? Why are you giving my administrative assistant a hard time, son?"

I said, "Mr. Hudson, I don't think the trouble I'm giving her is as difficult as what I had to go through to get down here. Please, sir, I usually don't beg. I just want a minute of your time."

He replied, "I can only give you one minute. I have a board meeting to attend."

As soon as I stepped into his office, I noticed a copy of the front-page article about me from the magazine, *Black Issues in Higher Education*. I said humbly, "Sir, my name is Michael Miller."

He said, "I know exactly who you are."

I responded, "I'm going to give it to you straight, no chaser. I've been awarded scholarship offers to several schools, including Yale, Duke, Johns Hopkins, and Florida State — all except Morehouse College. Sir, the bottom line is, that it's destined for me to go to this school. I've come to realize that Morehouse is where I need to be. Yes, I have many scholarship offers to many schools, but I need to be here. I can't wait on this

159

decision any longer. That's why I spontaneously drove twenty hours through a blizzard to get here."

He asked, "You really drove through that blizzard?"

I responded, "Yes, sir."

He said, "You must be crazy!"

I said, "I am. I'm also tired, sir. My body is exhausted. I can no longer wait to hear my fate. I'm tired of living the way I've been living, and I want to make a change in my life."

He said, "Okay. Well, how do you plan on paying a hundred thousand dollars to go to Morehouse College, Mr. Miller?"

I said, "Now, that's a good question! Well, I guess Morehouse is going to pay for it. I know this college doesn't offer transfer scholarships, but I'd love to have my matriculation funded by a scholarship from Morehouse College. I can't go back to Baltimore to finish my last semester and worry about paying for Morehouse College. Now, I know you think I'm crazy. That's because I am. Now, what's it going to be?"

He said, "Okay, I'll tell you what; give me till some time next week, and we'll see."

I said, "Ah, ah, no, no. I need to know this right now. I've been stressed out over this way too long, and I don't want to be just another phone call. Can we make this happen? Do we have a deal?"

He said, "You know what, Michael? I like your style. You are very bold, assertive, aggressive, confident, and straightforward. You've got a lot of heart to come in here and tell a man of my stature what you want. We need more men like you. It's quite evident that when you believe in something, you believe in going after it. Yes. We've got a deal!"

As I walked out the door, he concluded, "And by the way, don't ever let me see you again with your pants hanging off your behind. The next time you come, I want you to dress more appropriately, with a dress shirt, a tie, and a suit. You're going to have to get used to it here at Morehouse College. It's normal decorum, son."

I said, "Yes, sir."

I couldn't believe it. Spontaneously driving through the blizzard had paid off after all. I felt like the happiest man in the world. For the first time in my life, I could be assertive and bold, just like I was back on the streets, and get what I wanted.

Thanks, Oprah!

Oprah Winfrey once said, "When you empower a Morehouse Man, you empower the world." Never did I think that she was going to empower me, as well. When I reached the top of South Carolina on my way back to Baltimore, I received a phone call on my cell phone from Jim Henry, the president of the D. C., Morehouse alumni chapter. He said, "Michael, I've got some good news for you. Where are you?"

I said, "I'm in South Carolina, just coming from Morehouse College, and I've got some good news to tell you, too."

He said, "What are you doing at Morehouse?"

I said, "It's a long story. I'll tell you later."

He said, "Well, let me go first. I just got off the phone with someone who's pretty impressed with you. The bottom line is that the generosity of Oprah Winfrey is going to pay for your entire education at Morehouse College."

161

I said, "You gotta be kidding me."

I pulled the car onto the shoulder and pinched myself to make sure I wasn't dreaming. After that, I couldn't hear a word he was saying. I didn't want to be rude, so I thanked him for calling me and told him I would see him when I got back to Baltimore to thank him in person.

As I sat there, all I could do was ask the question, "Why me? Why would anyone want to invest up to a hundred-thousand dollars on my education (the four year cost to attend Morehouse College)?"

Then a voice spoke to me and said, "Why not you?" It was a very overpowering emotional feeling; I'd received double portions for my trouble.

The Making of a Man, a Morehouse Man

The rites of passage at Morehouse College taught me that a male is what you are when you are *born*, but a man is what you have to *become*. I just knew that my age, being a single parent, paying my own bills, and taking care of my manly responsibilities encapsulated my manhood. But while I was a man in training, Morehouse College stressed the importance of not just walking, talking, and looking like a man; I had to *be* a man. I had to think like a man. I had to be educated like a man. And I had to show them that I was a man.

I initially resented their philosophy of how a true man is supposed to be. This made me furious, and I was ready to take the next plane back home. I asked myself, *Who are they to tell me whether I'm a man or not? They don't know me! I'm already a man! I take care of myself!* But it was at Morehouse where I learned that a boy could become a sperm donor but not necessarily a man or a father. Once you understand the concept of responsibility and the transformation from boyhood to manhood, only then are you able to make the transition into your manhood.

At Morehouse, it became important for me to finish everything that I had started but not completed. Now that I was undergoing my manhood rites of passage, spiritually, educationally, mentally, as well as physically, I had to go back and make everything right. I had to atone for every wrong which I had committed and for every person whom I had harmed. All, not some, of my crooked paths had to be made straight.

In Search of My Destiny

While I was still at Morehouse, I made the bold decision to see if I had fathered any other children besides Dévon. Even if they already had an acting father, I wanted to accept my responsibility as a man. To find out if I had any other children, I sought out every woman I potentially could have had children with, and I ordered DNA tests.

I believed that to *reach* my destiny, I had to *find* my destiny. I was both unaware and unsatisfied, and until I fulfilled my desire to know if I had any other children, I felt incomplete.

Many men get this notion but choose to ignore it. We go on with our lives as if we hadn't left anything behind — especially children. We pretend to be happy, but we're not whole. We run away from the truth. How can we be men by claiming that

163

we are fathers — and still ignore the possibility that we may have more children who we haven't acknowledged? We're just running from the responsibility and financial obligation which comes with raising children. We complain about the little bit of money that we send the mothers for child support, worried that we can't afford the car payments or the mortgage payments, but we still dress like we want to. But making a difference in a child's life is far more important than what we drive, where we live, or what we wear on our backs.

Many people told me that I was just asking for trouble in my search for my abandoned children. A former girlfriend, Rhonetta, initially put up a fight. She stated on several occasions that her son's father was also her daughter's father. Although I didn't know the daughter's name at the time, I continued to fight to see if I was actually her father.

A few years later, I found out that the young girl's assumed father had died, and that was the perfect time to try to convince Rhonetta to arrange a DNA test to see if I was the biological father. After years trying to convince me that I wasn't the father, she finally gave in. The Circuit Court of Baltimore City warned me that if the girl wasn't my child, I would still have to pay for all the DNA fees and other costs associated with bringing this case before the court. And if she was my child, I would have to pay the past child-support payments and medical expenses which had resulted from her mother being on welfare for the past few years. It was roughly fifteen-thousand dollars, but again, I really didn't care. All that mattered was a little girl who could be growing up without a dad. I wanted to know if I was her father or not.

On the day of my court hearing, a woman walked into the courtroom. The little girl with her stopped what she was doing and began to gaze into my eyes. Then she started smiling. She was cute, cuddly, and chubby. I said to myself, *What fool in his right mind would neglect a precious, little girl like this? He must be crazy. Can't he see that she really needs all of the support she can get?* I really felt sorry for this little girl because of the condition that she was in. But this did not stop me from having a friendly conversation with her.

I took her hand and asked her, "What's your name?"

"Destiny," she said.

I looked down at my court papers and saw that the little girl in the court case was named Destiny, too. *This can't be her,* I thought.

We had a lot of fun, laughing and playing together for about fifteen minutes, and having a good time! As I continued to have even more fun with her, it saddened me to know that her real dad would be coming soon to take her away. I then handed her back to the woman who I thought was her mom.

Rhonetta walked into the courtroom and said, "Oh, hi, Mike. This is Destiny, and this is my sister, Cherita."

I said to myself, "I've found my Destiny!"

As soon as my case came up, the judge declared that I was indeed the father of Destiny, based on the DNA evidence (99.98 percent). I instantly left the courthouse and took her shopping to start fulfilling my role as her dad. Unfortunately, her mom had not been seeing to the welfare of my daughter. Destiny's hair wasn't being combed, and her hygiene wasn't being tended to.

165

Reclaiming My Destiny

In my opinion, Rhonetta's home and neighborhood was rampant with drugs and was not conducive for raising a child. So, I decided to fight for custody of my daughter, as well. This custody battle was not as difficult as had been the one for the custody of my son. Rhonetta had other "issues" going on in her life, which made it a lot easier to fight for custody of my daughter. Later, I was awarded full custody of Destiny. Now, I was a single parent of both Destiny and Dévon.

Raising my daughter as a single parent was a bit more challenging than raising my son. I had to be more affectionate and less militant. Although having a son calls for affection and attention, I had to give Destiny more hugs, more kisses, more cuddling, more "I love you, baby." You know, all of that mushy stuff.

According to researcher, Sonora Dodd, "Fathers play crucial roles in their children's lives. Ideally, they teach them love, respect, and discipline. A father's relationship with his daughter is often the best predictor of whether she will grow up to have a lasting, fulfilling relationship with her own spouse. A father's relationship with his son is critically important to the development of self-discipline and a healthy, respectful attitude toward women."

Children whose fathers are involved in their lives tend to do better in school, are less prone to depression, and are more successful in relationships.

166

Adam, Adam, Where Art Thou?

Some fathering advocates would say that almost every social ill faced by America's children is related to being fatherless. As supported by the data below, "Children from fatherless homes are more likely to be poor, become involved in drug and alcohol abuse, drop out of school, and suffer from health and emotional problems. Boys are more likely to become involved in crime, and girls are more likely to become pregnant as teens."

According to a study conducted by the U.S. Department of Health and Human Services in 2004, a father's absence is often accompanied by psychological consequences for his children, which include "higher-than-average levels of youth suicide, low intellectual and educational performance, and higher-than-average rates of mental illness, violence, and drug use." Sixty-three percent of teen suicides are related to the absence of a father. Ninety percent of all homeless and runaway children are related to the absence of a father. Seventy-five percent of all adolescent patients in chemical-abuse centers come from fatherless homes.

As these disturbing statistics show, it is important for fathers to be there for their children. I remember when Dévon first came home to live with me. He misbehaved in ways that some eight-year-old children do, such as lying, stealing, and being disruptive in school. Realizing that providing for him was not enough, by second nature, I began to raise him as I had been raised, and doing what my parents did.

I wouldn't tell him why I was punishing him. Whenever he acted up, I would just spank him or holler at him, hoping

167

that the punishment would teach him to behave. But just as I had perceived the spankings as someone there to *beat* me but not *teach* me, he thought I was just hurting him.

I was just imitating what my parents, who believed in "Spare the rod, spoil the child," had done to me. I thought that these principles were instructed by God. But that phrase is nowhere in the Bible; I couldn't even find a biblical verse that was close to it. It was just a cliché. What the Bible does say is that constant discipline is the key: Proverbs 13:24 says, *"He who spares his rod hates his son, but he who loves him disciplines him promptly."*

Like my parents, I had good intentions, but I was using the wrong technique. An old adage in the African-American community says, "Everything ain't for everybody." Clearly, beating Dévon wasn't working for either of us, so I began to try other alternatives, starting with hugging, to show him that I loved him.

A Piece of the Puzzle

A father had just settled into his recliner on Sunday afternoon, looking forward to reading through his newspaper, when his five-year-old son Pookie came into the room. "Daddy! Daddy!" said the boy, "Can you play with me?"

The father then responded in a calm manner, "Son, Daddy wants to read his paper for a little while. But if you come back in twenty minutes, we can play together."

Pookie then grumbled out of the room, leaving his dad alone to read his paper. But five year olds have a poor sense of time. It was only a few minutes before Pookie came back and asked, "Daddy, can we play now?"

"Not now, Pookie," said the father. "Don't bother me until I'm finished with reading my paper." Pookie stomped his way out of the room to wait, but before his dad could even get to the sports section, Pookie returned. He pushed his head up under the paper and said, "Please, Daddy, can we play now?"

Now convinced that he would never get a moment's peace without giving in, the father looked on the floor and observed that there was a full-page map of the world included in his newspaper. With scissors, he started to cut the map into many pieces. He then took his son to the kitchen table, grabbed the scissors and some tape, gave it all to his son, and said, "Since I know how much you like jigsaw puzzles, I am going to give you the world all cut into pieces so that you can repair it all by yourself. When you finish putting together the puzzle of the world, then I'll play with you," his father promised. He knew it would take his son a long time to put the puzzle together, which would give him plenty of time to read his paper.

Not five minutes had passed, when his son burst back into the room with, "Daddy, Daddy, I'm through with the puzzle! Can we play now?"

"What? You're finished already?" asked the father. He got up from his chair and went into the kitchen to look. Indeed, the puzzle was complete, with every piece in its proper place. "Son, how did you do this so fast? You didn't know where the world was. How did you do it?" asked the father in astonishment.

And the child answered, "It was easy, Daddy. I didn't know how the world was supposed to look, but on the back of the map was the shape of a man. So I turned each little piece

169

and decided to put the man together first. When I had fixed the man, I turned it to the other side, and the whole world seemed to fit right into place."

The world we live in is, indeed, broken and urgently needs to be put back together. The only way to put a broken world together is by putting men back together who have been broken. Adam, Adam, where are you? If you change your life, men, it will result in a changed world. And when men begin to put their lives back together, the whole world will seem to fit right into place.

Chapter 10
Faith:
How I Got Over

"Faith is like electricity. You can't see it, but you can see the light."

—Anonymous

faith - *noun* or *verb*. belief that does not rest on logical proof or material evidence.

Faith in God was the foundation for my parents' perseverance in keeping our family together and continuing to raise us on their own. Family members and neighbors talked about us, laughed at us, and teased us. They often looked at us in shock and confusion as if to say, "I don't know how they did it." Even today, we're known as "The Miller family that made it."

All of my brothers and sisters graduated from high school, are all successful in their careers, and all are happily married. To their great credit, my parents raised these successful children with no welfare and no after-school programs. They didn't lose any of them to drugs, and none of them ever spent a night in jail. According to modern social scientists, we should have been doomed to failure, but by the Grace of God we somehow managed to beat the odds. We were supposed to be a dysfunctional family with six African-American men in prison, dead, or addicted to drugs. None of us succumbed to any of these negatives. The three women were supposed to have had a lot of children whom they couldn't take care of. Instead, two of my sisters had one child each and the third has two, all of whom are doing exceptionally well.

But had it not been for the Grace of God, and my parents' steadfast faith, there's no telling where we would all have ended up. My mother would kneel at the head of her bed and call on the name of the Lord, fervently asking God to protect us, lead us, and guide us during those desperate times. My father, as a deacon in our church, always made sure he took a parenthetical pause to pray for his family during altar call, "Lawd, watch over my chil'ren, even when dey go astray, Lawd, wheel 'em back into de ark of safety. Father God, bless my chil'ren one by one. Help 'em, Lawd, to understand, Lawd, dat in times of trouble ta jus' lean on you." My parents' strong religious faith led me to believe that "trouble wouldn't last always." Even when I went astray, I always knew that my parents prayed for me. Even when I cursed God, out of anger, I still believed that

172

He existed. This faith played a major role in my life. I was always God-conscious about my transgressions.

My Mama Prayed for Me!

The only method of punishment that my mother knew was the one that had been passed down to her from generation to generation: frequent beatings for frequent misbehavior. By the time I was in middle school, she was getting tired of beating me and receiving no results, so she finally looked to the hills from which cometh her help, God.

One day I was sent home from middle school for fighting a classmate and cursing out a teacher. I just *knew* that I was going to get a beating, but when I arrived, my mom was so drained from my misbehavior that as soon as I walked through the door, she took me by the hand and tears poured down her face like a mighty stream. I could tell that she was fed up with my ways and fed up with trying to beat some sense into me. Her confidence in her disciplining methods was taking a toll on her mental and physical health *and* her self-esteem as a mother, so she turned to God for help. Enough was enough. She had taken me as far as she could. It was time to impart the power of prayer.

She took me by the hand and told me to kneel with her at the foot of her bed. I didn't know what was going on. Tears rolled from her eyes, and she looked puzzled and confused as she cried out, "Peace, be still!"

I had caused her so much pain and anguish that she cried out loud and clear, "Father, I stretch out my hands to Thee, for there is no other help that I know!" She mourned and wept,

173

"God, if I ever needed You before, I sure do need You right now! Lawd, this one child, Michael, just can't seem to get right."

It had only been about ten minutes, but it seemed as if we were praying together for an hour. My mother went into her metaphysical state where she walked around the room, lifting up her hands and shouting, "Thank ya, Jesus! Thank ya! I claim this child in the name of Jesus!" Then she transferred in the middle of her prayer and talked to the Devil, and said, "Devil, I rebuke you! Get out of my house!"

I was kneeling there, just wondering when it was going to end. She returned to praying, holding me even tighter by the hands and shouting, "In the name of Jesus, I claim victory over my son, right now! God, for every sin he has committed, I cast it into the sea of forgiveness! I claim victory over his misbehaving in school! Whatever he can't get right, make it right! Whatever seems to have grabbed hold of 'im, loosen it, Lawd!" She finally closed her prayer with her seal of approval, "Let the words of my mouth, and the meditation of my heart, be always acceptable in thy sight, Amen!"

This moment was very spooky to me. My mother was a firm believer in the power of prayer, but I was confused about what was going on. That was the first and only time that she took me by the hand to pray with me. After that, she stopped giving me whippings and became a little more lenient toward me. I will never forget that day for the rest of my life.

Manifestation of Prayer

My mother's strange behavior as she prayed for me imparted a lesson that she couldn't teach me through physical punishment. I understood that she would rely on her spirituality to finish the race of raising me.

On the other hand, I felt that her prayer for me was in vain, because I didn't change immediately. I got into trouble again in school for my disruptive conduct. I remember questioning my mother during her new leniency tactics. When I came home, she started talking to me instead of beating me. I contradicted her by saying, "You see, Mama, that prayer that you had for me last week didn't even work."

Her response was, "He may not come when you want Him to come, but He's an on-time God; yes, He is!"

Time went by and I didn't see any change for the next ten years. I asked myself, *Does prayer really change things, or is it all a hoax?*

Hold on to that thought.

Many of us try to overburden ourselves with issues that are bigger than we are. The race that you are running may be going at a faster pace than you expected it to be. Don't rush; just pace yourself. We need to learn how to wait for God to manifest Himself so that we know how fast to run our race.

As I got older and my life began to miraculously change for the better, I asked my mother, "Why did God take so long to answer your prayer?"

She looked at me with a smile and said, "Michael, God answered my prayer the first day I prayed. It was just ten years later when it was manifested."

Though she didn't routinely grab us by the hand and pray, my mother often knelt down at the head of the bed to pray for her children. I believe her prayers are the only reason why my brothers and sisters and I have made it this far in life.

One of the key components of faith is to always be optimistic. Many times, people will subconsciously speak healing within themselves. They will say things like, "I'm going through hell." The key word is that you are going *through* hell and you are not *in Hell*. While you are going through hell, just keep going. Soon you will get to your destination.

After being fired by Notre Dame, the first African-American coach, Tyrone Willingham, said, "I have never had a bad day. I have had bad moments, and sometimes, those bad moments will run into another day — okay? — that'll have hurt, pain, etc. But it's still a good day. There are many blessings that Tyrone Willingham has."

Your faith will help you to overcome many obstacles in your life. It's very important that you not yield to your feelings but rely on your faith. For example, when someone asks how you feel, say to them, "I don't live by *feelings*; I live by *faith*." And your faith throughout your journey in life will see you through.

Nelson Mandela went from being a *prisoner* to being a *president*, all because he had faith! Benjamin Banneker built and laid out Washington D.C. as if it was a Masonic temple, all because he had faith! Harriet Tubman led many slaves to freedom through the Underground Railroad, all because she had faith! Mary McLeod Bethune went down to a junkyard in Daytona, Florida, and said, "I'm going to build me a college here." Now Bethune-Cookman College is one of the leading African-American institutions, all because Mary McLeod Bethune had faith!

Give It to God

Your life mission can't be completed by human power alone. At some point during the race in your life, you will have to rely on God for you to make it through your difficult and arduous journey. In fact, that's the ONLY way to make it through. You will have to trust and believe that if God allowed you to go *to* it, He will bring you *through* it. He will equip you with everything that you need in your life's race. You just have to rely on Him. In other words, where God *guides*, He *provides*. He can take a talent, an opportunity, a skill, or a hobby and use it as part of your life mission to help other people, but you've got to rely on God.

You may say, "Mike, it's too late for me!"

My response is simple: The race isn't over yet. It's never too late! It's not how you start the race that matters, but how you finish. Keep your faith in your race! Surely, your faith will see you through to completion!

You Gotta Have Crazy Faith!

My experiences have taught me that while you're on your journey in life, it's all right to be crazy. In the race of life, you often worry about how many people are in front of you, how you look, your facial expressions, or how many miles you have to go. If you're crazy, you won't worry about stuff like that. In fact, I think insanity is worrying about something that you have no control over, anyway.

You must let God do what He says He's going to do, regardless of how bad the situation may seem. Very soon, He will step in and work things out in your favor, if you believe. Learn how to be a little crazy sometimes to go by what you can't see and still believe it deep within your heart, even if everyone around you says that it isn't possible. You will have to go against the grain of what society determines you can and cannot do.

Unfortunately, we live in a society that prides itself on research data, rather the willpower of human beings working together with spiritual power. If research dictates or declares that it's impossible, we're left to believe that it can't be done. If no one has done what you're trying to do before, or if it's not thought of as "humanly possible," it may seem impossible for you to reach your goal, mainly because we live in a society that lacks spirituality.

There was a story about a woman in California whose car flipped over on a slippery road. Consequently, her infant son was pinned beneath it. The 3,700 pound car was no match for the love for her son, though. Defying all odds, she elevated the car with all of the "crazy faith" that she possessed, and her son crawled from under the car to safety. Though it didn't make logical sense, given the size of her frail body frame, her insanity helped her in her desperate time of trouble. It was a life-or-death situation on the line. When it came to saving her beloved son, her mind gave her body the willpower, resilience, and might of many men.

There are many people who have benefited from using their insanity in a sane society. If they'd had an ounce of doubt or had used their "sanity," they would've failed a long time ago. Instead, they channeled their energy to concentrate on developing the necessary power to meet unbearable circumstances.

Insanity has several definitions. For instance, according to Einstein, "Insanity is doing the same thing over and over again and expecting different results." One wise man once said, "Only the insane have strength enough to survive. Only the survivors determine what is sane." Others have said that insanity is trying to make reality conform to your views, rather than conforming your views to reality.

I'm Crazy!

Had I listened to the teachers, some family members, and friends, who said that I couldn't make reality conform to my views, my dreams would have been shattered. Instead, I went through a period where I just became insane. Quite frankly, I'm still crazy, which is not bad at all.

I was crazy enough to go inside a classroom where most of the students were fresh out of high school, knowing I had overcome illiteracy just two months before enrolling in college. I was crazy to declare, against my advisor's recommendation, that I was not only going to graduate with my Associate of Arts degree, but I was going to do it at the record pace of a year and a half, with honors, a goal that seemed impossible, especially for a student with my background.

After surmounting my first obstacle, I was crazy enough to consider taking on the challenge of going to the prestigious Morehouse College in Atlanta, Georgia — where my critics said that I wouldn't have the same support that the community college was giving me; instead, I would be on my own.

As more haters continued to criticize me for biting off more than I can chew, I respond, "I don't mind biting off more than I can chew. I'm hungry!"

Many people used to say things like, "Why not go to a local school? Why do you have to be such a big shot and take a risk like that? You're setting yourself up for failure." I remember when one college president, whose school was not one of my top choices, called me and tried to recruit me for his university. When I told him my final choices, he said, "Mr. Miller, it's better to be a big fish in a little pond than to be a little fish in a big pond." I guess I was supposed to respond with fear, take the shortcut, and settle for second best. It made perfectly good sense to follow his advice and not be a little fish in a big pond, huh? But instead of giving in, I responded, "Sir, it doesn't matter, because I love to swim."

I was crazy enough, at times, to take twenty-four credits per semester. However, the obstacles that I was surmounting weren't about me; they were about the next students who came along with a past like mine. I challenged myself to give them hope that they could do it, also.

180

I had the same routine every day. I would go to school, go to work, come home and be a single parent, study, check my goal sheet to make sure that I was on track, pray, and then go to bed. I wasn't missing out on anything by giving up my old lifestyle for my new one. The people who were in the clubs before I went to college were the same people who were in the clubs when I graduated. So, it wasn't like I was really missing anything at all.

Because an insane person does things over and over again, I didn't want to keep my sanity. Being sane would have made me declare that doing all things was impossible and that I couldn't do what I had set out to do. I didn't even want to be around sane people. Sane people look at what is real or possible, but I didn't care about that.

If you want to finish your race, be crazy! I'm crazy enough to have faith when things look bleak. I'm crazy enough to walk by faith and not by sight. I'm crazy enough to believe that my condition is not my conclusion. I'm crazy enough to still believe that even in my dark, dismal, and difficult destitution, everything is going to be okay, regardless of my situation. You have to be crazy enough to believe that. If not, instead of walking by *faith*, you will walk by how you *feel*. Instead of having *fortitude*, you will *faint*. Instead of believing that you have divine *favor*, you will believe that you are a *failure*. Soon, and very soon, you will learn that the only thing you need in the face of adversity is faith! That's it!

New Level, New Devils

With each new lap of your race, you may suffer increased attacks to test your faith. With each new blessing, spiritual

181

attacks seem to increase. When God takes you to a new level, there will always be new challenges and obstacles in your way. Once you move to a new level in your life, there will be more obstacles which will come against you.

As you settle into your new place and face every type of adversity which may come your way, remember that God has already determined your path to the destiny that He is sending you.

The curious thing was, that when I was wasting my life away, nobody cared. However, as soon as I decided to do something with my life, I constantly came under attack from the "new devils". As I moved from having my GED to attending a two-year college, there were family and friends who would say, "Michael is going to school? Oh, he's not going to finish. He won't stay in for long. As always, he'll drop out soon."

Some would even be bold enough to say to my face, "Michael, how are you going to go to college when you've been out of school all these years? Why are you going to embarrass yourself like that? How can you have the nerve to be in a classroom with a bunch of high-school graduates?"

I would respond boldly and confidently, "Keep talking." While they were *talking*, I was *walking* into my destiny. When I started taking courses at Baltimore City Community College, I had newer devils. Colleagues and co-workers would congregate and attempt to kill my resilient spirit.

I once heard someone say, "The only reason he is doing good here is because this is a community college. He'll never do that at a four-year college, especially an honors institution like Morehouse College."

I would respond, "Keep talking!"

I then went to Morehouse College to continue my matriculation. While I was there, I was inspired by the words of Dr. Mays, "You've got to run *twice* as fast or forever be left behind." And that was exactly what I did. I graduated from Morehouse, too, at a record pace of a year and a half with honors.

Just when I thought that I'd done enough to shut my lower-level devils up, there was always some new devils coming along, finding something new to talk about, "Well, he has his Bachelor's Degree from Morehouse College, but he can't do it in grad school."

As always, I would respond, "Keep talking!"

Then, I continued to study at other prestigious universities on a graduate level. Even after receiving my Master's Degree, and now being a PhD candidate, some new difficulty would always present itself. You would've thought that the critics would realize by now that the more they had to say, the more they motivated me. Scholars of rap music would call it "Making your haters your motivators."

As I climbed the ladder, I had to learn how to move on from "Keep talking" to "This, too, shall pass." There is a story about a poisonous snake that crawled into the cockpit of a plane before takeoff. The passengers were alarmed, but the pilot didn't seemed to be worried about the snake. He ignored the passengers' concern and kept flying the plane to higher altitudes. To the passengers' surprise, the snake was dead. The pilot explained that he knew that if he just flew the plane high enough, the snake wouldn't be able to stand the higher altitude.

After flying higher and higher, you will notice that, at some point, the snake must die. As you continue to fly, take the time to thank your critics for their tenacious efforts to bring you down. Continue to thank them for their jealousy, their envy, and their deceit. You will need it to get you to the next level. It will only serve to make you stronger as you climb the ladder of success. It will only be fuel to your faith.

Chapter 11
The Journey of Self-Discovery: *Who Am I?*

"When I discover who I am, I'll be free."
                                        —Ralph Ellison

self-discovery - *noun*. the act or process of achieving understanding or knowledge of oneself.

When I realized that I was destined to win the race of life, I set out on a joyful journey to discover who I was really destined to be.

There is a story told of a man who lost his keys inside his house but decided to look for them outside. His neighbor came by and asked, "Have you lost something?" The man said, "My keys," and asked his neighbor to help him find them. After some minutes of searching and turning up nothing, the neighbor asked him, "Are you sure you lost the keys here?" The man replied, "No, I didn't lose them here." The neighbor asked, "Well, where did you lose them?" The man replied, "Inside the house." The neighbor asked, "If you lost your keys inside the house, why are you looking for them out here?" The man responded, "Because it's dark inside my house. There's more light out here." The moral of the story is: the keys to your life will not be found in the light of the world but in the darkness of your soul. Acknowledgment of your dark side brings light. Besides, the darkroom is necessary for any good picture to get developed.

To discover yourself and become whole, you must acknowledge and accept your dark side. No matter what you've done in the past, you can change your behavior today. You did the best you thought you could; now it's time to do better and finish what you've started. To do that, you must begin by going into those dark places of your life.

I tried to avoid writing this book for more than six years. I didn't want to acknowledge the dark side of my life. When I finally attempted to write this book, I was met with great resistance from within myself. It was a very difficult and tedious race from start to finish. I had to conjure up old feelings about my past. I would finally write a page, walk away crying, and then go at it again. Then I would write a single sentence, and then walk away again because I was so overwhelmed with the emotions of my past. Then, I would stop writing altogether, attempting to run away from the pain. It was an atrocious, painful, and arduous battle. Yet later, after hundreds of typed pages, I finished my race by writing this book!

Hurt People, Hurt People

One of the most important things that I've learned about myself through self-discovery is that hurt people, hurt people. Because I was hurting inside, I hurt everyone that tried to love me. All I needed to hear was those magic words of, "I love you" and that was it. I now had to hurt you, before you hurt me, all because it was too reminiscent to those who supposedly love me, but consequently hurt me. Until fairly recently, I could never understand why I hurt so many of my past girlfriends. It was because they were trying to love me. And I wouldn't just ordinarily hurt them. *No.* I would hurt them to almost beyond repair. I was the type of guy that would hurt females and make them hate men.

My daughter Brianna's mother, Nikki, really has felt the wrath of my pain. I was only eighteen years old but was filled with rage. The more she tried to love me, I tried equally as hard to hurt her. I remember taking her to the top of the stairs and threatening to kill her. Why? I don't know. I was just mad at life — mad about living. So, I punched a whole into the window, took out a piece of the glass from the window, held the glass to her neck, and threaten to kill her. I knew something was wrong with me when her eyes began to roll into the back of her head and I acted as if I didn't care. I just kept saying, "B_tch, I'm gonna kill ya!"

We constantly fought, or should I say, I fought her, because of the pain that I was feeling. I believe this is the reason why so many African-American men are hurting the loved ones they are with. I think that it is essentially because they are truly hurting inside. The thug image that many of them try to portray is just a

187

façade. What is really on the inside is that pain that they are afraid to share with their significant others. Many come from broken families where either the father wasn't there, the mother was on drugs, or even both, or they are confused about how to deal with the everyday stress of life, etc. Consequently, when we are hurting, we hurt. So hurt people do hurt people. It is only when hurt people have been *healed*, they can *help* people.

The Manifestation of My Problems

I've finally realized, through self-discovery, that the things I had thought were my problems really weren't my problems. Hanging out on the corners was not my problem. Not being a father to my son was not my problem. My early childhood was not my problem. Partying all the time was not my problem. Smoking marijuana and drinking alcohol was not my problem. Being disruptive in school and being a class clown was not my problem. Anger was not my problem. Having low self-esteem was not my problem. And finally, my rage with God was not my problem.

These were all just manifestations of my problems, and I had to deal with these problems from the inside out. My problem was that I couldn't set myself free, because I never knew who I really was. I thought I was hard, but I was really crying out for help. I thought I was a thug, but I was really a thinker. I thought I was a man, but I was still only a male. Once I was able to change my childish and juvenile mind-set, I was then able to change my self-concept.

Changing Your Self-Concept

Changing your self-concept can be painful because of the battle that will commence in your mind between the 'old you' and the 'new you'. Also, you will struggle with others whom you used to bow down to, whereas, now you're speaking and standing up for yourself. Then, they'll accuse you of thinking that you're better than everybody else, and make comments like, "You think that you're a cut above the rest. You think you're all that and a bag of chips," or "You think that you're God's gift to the world."

Actually, that is because you *are*! You *are* all that! The Bible declares, "You are a royal priesthood, a chosen generation." You *are* a child of the Most High, the King (God). Hence, you *are* an heir to the Throne. If you're a child of the King, that automatically makes you a prince or a princess.

Some people will try to bring you down because of their own self-hatred, but you must remain steadfast. When I started standing up for myself and what I believed in, the people around me started feeling uncomfortable because they had become so comfortable with the old me. Change is very uncomfortable, so you must get comfortable with being uncomfortable.

"Who you are" is not predicated on what other people think of you. "Who you are" is not about your address or what community you live in. "Who you are" is not predicated on your last name. "Who you are" is not about what you used to do or whether you had a father in the house or not. It is, rather, predicated on understanding that you are a child of God. That's it!

Being a child of God inevitably makes you more than wonderful, regardless of what society says. My mother used to say it plain and simple, "I am what I am; I is what I is, and I'm gonna be what I'm gonna be. Not because of who I am, but because of *Whose* I am!"

Are We There Yet?

Every parent who has taken a long journey with a child is familiar with the question, "Are we there yet?"

Like those children, I was on a journey, but I was not there yet. I was *better*, but I hadn't yet reached *best*. Most people are so glad to be *better* that they give up on being their *best*. They fail to take advantage of the opportunity for true greatness because they settle for mediocrity and are often afraid to think outside the box.

"Well, I'm better," they say to themselves, "and *something* is better than *nothing*. At least, I'm making ends meet, but I'm barely getting by."

And you are right, you are barely getting by, but that is not better, that is second best. I do not believe that God has brought us this far along the way to barely get us by.

Don't Worry, Be Happy!

Too often, we choose to worry rather than choosing to be happy. The word '*worry*' comes from the Old English word '*wyrgan*', which means 'to strangle'.

Many times, we worry about things we shouldn't worry about. My mother used to tell me, "It ain't no use putting up your umbrella till it rains."

190

As long as I've got an umbrella in my hand, which is God, I have nothing to worry about, because I have that shield of protection over me. He will shelter me from the rain. The Word of God encourages us to avoid worrying about our physical needs like clothing and food. I believe that worrying is a sin, because when you worry, you're doubting God's capabilities. When you worry, you unconsciously diminish God to someone who can do *some* things but not *all* things. God will dispatch angels in a time of need, and because He knows our struggles, our pain, and our needs, we need not worry about anything. We're in God's Hands.

Our self-concept is also affected by our concept of happiness. Many people believe that if they can change their friends, spouse, or peers, they can enhance their self-esteem and consequently be happy. I take the simple approach: No one can make you happy; that's your responsibility.

When your happiness is determined by the fate of someone else, then you have given him or her too much power and undue influence over you and your unconscious mind. That is too much power for anyone to have over you. When you are not doing what you want to do, you start to feel helpless, hopeless, and victimized. This causes you to be frightened and angry. Consequently, your happiness has been put on hold.

Dr. Charmaine Sanders writes:

"Happiness lives within us, never outside of us. Therefore, it cannot come from external sources. The joy we get from things outside is the cream on the cake, an extra bonus, but it can never be the whole story. Relying

191

on people, places, or events to make us happy is the ultimate fantasy. It can only bring transitory pleasure and disappointment in the end."

Where do I go from Here?

The journey of self-discovery can be a daunting task at times. However, you must be persistent to find which way to go. In the book, *Alice in Wonderland*, Alice comes to a fork in the road. While she stands there looking confused, the Cheshire cat grins facetiously, as if he knows something that she doesn't.

She asks the cat, "Would you tell me, please, which way I ought to go from here?"

"That depends a good deal on where you want to get to," says the cat.

Alice responds, "I don't much care where."

To which the cat replies, "Then it doesn't matter which way you go."

Possibly, like Alice, you are seeking a purpose and a direction. As you come to a crossroads in your journey through life, you may ask, like Alice, which way you should go from here. But if you don't know where you're going, it really doesn't matter in which direction you go.

You must continue to find "which way to go" to lead you to your destination. We can no longer sit around and wait for things to happen; we've got to make them happen!

I've learned that life is filled with crossroads which lead to diverse destinations. Like Alice, I've reached a crossroads, or rather, many crossroads. Unlike Alice, however, I now know where I'm going and the road that I must take.

After dropping out of high school, I embarked on an expedition that led me to college. The road to college led me to a remarkable educational experience. My education at Morehouse College exposed me to some of the greatest minds in the country. During this time, I was forced to answer questions that stimulated my intellect. Confronting and overcoming this challenge took me to other roads that I eventually had to cross.

Ralph Waldo Emerson once said, "Don't go where the path may lead; go instead where there is no path, and leave a trail." College has both challenged me and prepared me for the roads ahead. On the road of life, I am trying to leave a trail, become a compassionate leader, and become a good parent. My college experience took me a step closer to these goals.

Without goals, we are just like Alice — traveling without a purpose in life. Remember, a goal without a plan is nothing but a thought. As one scholar has said, "Those who fail to plan, plan to fail." We all have an innate gift which was given by God. We just have to continue to discover who we are and find out what our purpose is in life. We *all* have one.

In his book, *Live Your Dreams*, Les Brown wrote, "The richest place on the planet is not some diamond mine or oil field. It is a cemetery, because in the cemetery, we bury the inventions that were never produced, the ideas and dreams that never became reality, the hopes and aspiration that were never acted upon." Les Brown also stated that most people take their dreams to the grave with them because they're afraid. They don't feel worthy, or they listen to negative inner conversations instead of

193

creating their own circumstances for success and exercising the power to change their lives. However, if you block those voices from entering your mind, as Les Brown suggested, your talents — no matter how limited or undeveloped — will take you to many places you've never been before.

I once heard a minister say, "God repositions His presence." When He's up front, he *guides* you, but when He's in the back, he *guards* you. Before He released you to your destiny, He was guiding you to show you where to go. But when He saw that you were on the right track, He got behind you to guard you. Often, our circumstances can be so overwhelming that we can't see God. If God's Presence isn't plain to you, it doesn't mean that He's left you; it just means that He's guarding you.

Your journey on your road to self-discovery will equip and empower you for the race. You have one last lap to go. Your witnesses are still cheering for you. Keep running. Your fans are waiting for you to cross the finish line. *So what* if you may come in last place? The fans are still cheering for you. You still have the stamina to make it, because God is with you! How do you think you've made it this far? Surely, you didn't make it on your own. In fact, you would've given up a long time ago; instead, God gave you the power to persevere. One last lap to go and you'll be victorious. One last lap and you find out what you are made of. One last lap and you'll be able to say, "I hung in there until the end! I did it! I've finished my race!"

Chapter 12
Crossing the Finish Line

"When I found that I had crossed that line [the Mason-Dixon Line], I looked at my hands to see if I was the same person. There was such a glory over everything; the sun came like gold through the trees, and over the fields, and I felt like I was in Heaven."

—Harriet Tubman

the finish line - *noun.* a line indicating the location of the finish of a race.

O nce you cross that finish line, you join the club. You've earned your membership in the Affiliation of the Making of a Marathon Runner. Whether you've finished first, last, or somewhere in the middle, you belong to this elite group of individuals. Everything that follows is an extension of your victory. You've done it! In between the starting line and the finish line, while struggling and persevering, you transformed — you became a contender.

The finish line is still not the end; the finish line is the beginning of yet another race. Life is a sequence of races, a series of starting and finishing lines. With the start of the next race, though, you will be stronger, faster, and more determined. You will find yourself standing at many more starting lines, beginning many more races. And for these acts of inauguration, for these decisions to participate in life's race, you will be granted hope. Standing at a starting line, any starting line, gives you permission to hope. Simply garnering the courage to begin a task, to stand at its starting line, instills the precious notion of optimism. This optimism will drive you from race to race and will eventually convert into expectation. Soon you will *expect* success.

Crossing the starting line may be a noteworthy act of courage, but crossing the finish line is a beautiful act of faith. Faith, if you don't know it, is one of humanity's most powerful emotions. Faith is the wind which propels us forward when we are tired and weary and want nothing more than to retreat. Faith is the mighty emotion which conquers fear. Faith is the emotion which grants us victory over our past, over the demons in our souls, and over all of those voices who tell us what we can and cannot be.

If standing at the starting line gives you permission to dream, crossing the finish line gives you permission to plan. Crossing the finish line allows you to design your next success, and to plan for the realization of your next dream. The last step of the race is the first step of the rest of your life.

Hold On!

I'm reminded of a time when I was having a conversation on the phone with a friend of mine, Mrs. Jenkins, who had recently overcome many obstacles in her life. She suffered a devastating divorce which could have left her financially crippled and with no means of caring for her family. Her ex-husband, who was an undercover millionaire, had maneuvered a way to hide his funds and pay her nothing after their fifteen years of marriage. With nothing else left, she put it all into God's Hands and surrendered to His Will. Then she went on a mission to reclaim her life, her self-esteem, and her happiness. Now, all she wanted was the comfort of finally knowing that she was divorced. After a long, hard-fought, six-year court battle, she said to the judge, "Your honor, I'm sick and tired of all of this. I don't want anything. Just give me my divorce!" The judge looked confused for a moment by what seemed an obtuse request, but he granted her wish. She stumbled out of the courtroom in despair, with no sign of hope, no financial obligation from her ex-husband, no right to the home they had built together, nothing. All she had left was God's Will, which consistently said to her, "Hold on." Despite being raised in a poverty-stricken community, she had enormous goals for herself and her family. She had to move out of her home and into an apartment, but she still had aspirations. She managed to turn her life around within two years after her divorce. She had worked in someone else's shop for more than twenty years as a beautician, but on her road to recovery, she began to acknowledge her dream of one day opening up her own hair salon.

Of course, she met many obstacles on that journey. At first there was no money coming in to finance her dream. A deal gone

197

bad almost left her in shambles. But by following God's Will, which told her to hold on, she finally saw her dream come true and opened up an elegant hair salon with a stable staff. She bought a townhouse, which was ten times better than the home she had lost. Later, she purchased her dream house, a luxurious single-family home in a suburban community, three-times better and larger than her town home. She then remarried, but to an honorable and devoted gentlemen this time, who later added more happiness in her life.

In profound words of faith, she told me, "Michael, this is not the end to my beginning; this is the beginning of my beginning." She knew that more blessings were in store for her.

It appears that Mrs. Jenkins possessed the power and the potency of the lightening bug. What makes the lightning bug glow with its brilliant-green iridescence is a substance called autoluminescent protein. In other words, the bug doesn't need outside light to glow; it just glows from within itself with its internal light.

It's a creation of God; therefore, it glows in the presence *and* in the absence of other lightning bugs, just as you should glow in the presence *and* in the absence of your friends and family members. The lightning bug doesn't need any external support in order to turn on its inner light for everyone to see, and neither do you. It already has that capability in its biological make-up, and so do you. You must adopt the lightning-bug theory if you expect to finish your race in life. And when you do, make sure you take off flying and illuminate yourself, so that others can see and appreciate your light.

If you believe you can, you will. No matter what goal you set for yourself, always keep an image of the finish line in sight, and don't stop until you get there.

By finishing what you've started, you've found out that the easiest thing was *doing* it, but the hardest thing was *believing* that you could do it. Many people fail because they don't believe in themselves. Once you believe that nothing in the world can stop you from achieving your goals — except yourself — nothing in the world can stop you from reaching your destiny. Not trusting God or believing in my ability to finish school hindered me, just as the lack of faith and self-confidence prevents many people from reaching their goals.

What you do now is up to you. You've seen what you can do. If you've stuck with the training program, you've seen yourself filled with joy and blinded by frustration. You've overcome your fears. You've been humbled by both the strength and the fragility of your body. You've found what you thought were your limits, and you have gone beyond them.

You've also learned that what stops most of us from achieving our dreams — as athletes and as people — are the confines of our imaginations. We can never be more than we imagine we can be. And as long as we restrict ourselves by our imaginations, we forever bind ourselves to our past and blind ourselves to our futures.

Your limits now lie behind you. By taking that final step across the finish line, you have freed yourself from all of the things you ever thought you knew about yourself. By crossing the finish line, you have taken the very first step on the track to your life. Are you ready? Sure you are! Get up and win that race!

I leave you with an anonymous poem which continues to inspire me in my race in life. I hope it does the same for you.

199

The Race

Whenever I start to hang my head in front of failure's face,
my downward fall is broken by the memory of a race.
A children's race, young boys, young men; how I remember well,
excitement, sure, but also fear, it wasn't hard to tell.

They all lined up so full of hope, each thought to win that race
or tie for first, or if not that, at least take second place.
Their parents watched from off the side, each cheering for
their son, and each boy hoped to show his folks that he
would be the one.

The whistle blew and off they flew, like chariots of fire,
to win, to be the hero there, was each young boy's desire.
One boy in particular, whose dad was in the crowd, was
running in the lead and thought "My dad will be so proud."

But as he speeded down the field and crossed a shallow dip,
the little boy who thought he'd win, lost his step and slipped.
Trying hard to catch himself, his arms flew everyplace,
and midst the laughter of the crowd he fell flat on his face.

As he fell, his hope fell too; he couldn't win it now.
Humiliated, he just wished to disappear somehow.
But as he fell his dad stood up and showed his anxious face,
which to the boy so clearly said, "Get up and win that race!"

He quickly rose, no damage done, behind a bit that's all,
and ran with all his mind and might to make up for his fall.
So anxious to restore himself, to catch up and to win,
his mind went faster than his legs. He slipped and fell again.

He wished that he had quit before with only one disgrace.
"I'm hopeless as a runner now, I shouldn't try to race."
But through the laughing crowd he searched and found his
father's face with a steady look that said again,
"Get up and win that race!"

So he jumped up to try again, ten yards behind the last.
"If I'm to gain those yards," he thought, "I've got to run real fast!"
Exceeding everything he had, he regained eight, then ten. . .
but trying hard to catch the lead, he slipped and fell again

Defeat! He lay there silently. A tear dropped from his eye.
"There's no sense running anymore! Three strikes I'm out!
Why try?
I've lost, so what's the use?" he thought. "I'll live with my disgrace."
But then he thought about his dad, who soon he'd have to face.

"Get up," an echo sounded low, "you haven't lost at all,
for all you have to do to win is rise each time you fall.
Get up!" the echo urged him on, "Get up and take your place!
You were not meant for failure here! Get up and win that race!"

So, up he rose to run once more, refusing to forfeit,
  and he resolved that win or lose, at least he wouldn't quit.
So far behind the others now, the most he'd ever been,
  still he gave it all he had and ran like he could win.

Three times he'd fallen stumbling, three times he rose again.
  Too far behind to hope to win, he still ran to the end.
They cheered another boy who crossed the line and won first place,
  head high and proud and happy — no falling, no disgrace

But, when the fallen youngster crossed the line, in last place,
  the crowd gave him a greater cheer for finishing the race.
And even though he came in last with head bowed low, unproud,
  you would have thought he'd won the race, to listen to the crowd.

And to his dad he sadly said, "I didn't do so well."
  "To me, you won," his father said. "You rose each time you fell."
And now when things seem dark and bleak and difficult to face,
  the memory of that little boy helps me in my own race.

For all of life is like that race, with ups and downs and all.
  And all you have to do to win is rise each time you fall.
And when depression and despair shout loudly in my face,
  another voice within me says, "Get up and win that race!"

About the Author

Michael Miller delivers powerful messages that penetrate the minds of urban youth worldwide. His messages are clear and simple, yet provocative and well grounded. As one of the nation's most prolific and dynamic speakers, he motivates thousands of students and adult learners and travels extensively across the country, conducting lectures, workshops, and professional development training sessions. This scholar, motivational speaker, author, and lecturer is acclaimed by many media outlets as, "One of the future leaders of tomorrow."

In a matter of three years, he obtained his GED, A.A. degree, and a B.A. degree from Morehouse College and set a national record as the first person ever to do so.

In 2000, Miller was honored by Morehouse College as a *Beating the Odds* scholar. He was recognized for his efforts as a single parent, full-time student, and as a dedicated father with up to $100,000 to complete his matriculation through the benevolence of Oprah Winfrey. Michael Miller later received his Masters of Science in Psychology and is now a successful PhD candidate. He has received countless awards, including the Dr. Martin Luther King Jr. *Footsteps Award*, *Academic Achievement of the Year*, and *Father of the Year*. He was featured in the *Who's Who Among Students In America*. Above all, he was named Motivational Speaker and Writer of the Year for 2000-2003 by the *Speakers Bureau of America*.

204

Michael Miller has not forgotten his roots. He continues to give back to his Baltimore community. He is the Founder and President of the *Beating the O.D.D.S. Foundation,* through which students are mentored and awarded scholarships to attend college to further their education. Through his leadership, over thirty new youth and adult literacy scholarships and programs have been established nationwide. As the US Ambassador for Adult Education, Miller is a beacon of hope who travels extensively, empowering young people with advice such as: "It doesn't matter where you start; what counts is where you decide to finish."

Feel free to contact Michael Miller at
Amorehouseman2000@yahoo.com

Order Form

Name_____

Company Name_____

Address_____

City:_____State:_____Zip:_____

Telephone: (___) _____Email:_____

Please send me _____copies of **A Promise to Persevere**

Price   **Shipping**:   **Total**
$15.99 $3.50 per book $19.49
Sales Tax: Add 5% to books shipped to Maryland addresses.

Check____   Money Order____   Cashiers Check_____

Total enclosed: $_____

Make payable and send to:
Empowerment Press Publishing Company
P.O. Box 794
Ellicott City, MD.   21041-794

Please allow 7 days for delivery.

***

Books are available at special discounts for bulk purchases, sales promotion, fundraising or educational purposes.

For more information write to:
Empowerment Press Publishing Company
PO Box 794
Ellicott City, MD.
21041-794
USA

Or visit our website at
www.apromisetopersevere.com